Robert B. Waltz

# *Romancing the Ballad:*
### *How Orpheus the Minstrel became King Orfeo*

Occasional Papers in Folklore
No. 3

Robert B. Waltz

# *Romancing the Ballad:*
### How Orpheus the Minstrel became King Orfeo

Waltz, Robert B. Romancing the Ballad. S.l.:
Loomis House, 2013. Print.

© 2013 by Robert B. Waltz

CAMSCO Music
145 Hickory Corner Rd., E. Windsor, NJ 08520
www.camscomusic.com

Loomis House Press
www.loomishousepress.com

ISBN 978-1-935243-86-1

Edited by Ed Cray (cray@usc.edu)
and Susan O. Friedman (sofridman@verizon.net)

Cover illustration: Detail of Orpheus among the Thracians, from an Attic red-figure vase ( ca. 440 BCE).

πρός
Ἐλίζαβεθ Ῥώσενβεργ
ῥοδῇ ἀληθινή ἐν τῇ ἐρήμῳ

*(to Elizabeth Rosenberg,*
*a true rose in the wilderness)*

*And who might of his harping hear*
*He should think that he were*
*In one of the joys of paradise —*
*Such joy and melody in his harping is.*
                    —*Sir Orfeo, lines 19-22, modernized*

## CONTENTS

| | |
|---|---:|
| *Acknowledgments* | 1 |
| *Preface* | 3 |
| CHAPTER 1 *The Beginnings of Romance* | 4 |
| CHAPTER 2 *The Original Orpheus Myth* | 11 |
| CHAPTER 3 *The Romance Sir Orfeo* | 14 |
| CHAPTER 4 *The Ballad "King Orfeo"* | 26 |
| CHAPTER 5 *Comparing the Versions* | 31 |
| CHAPTER 6 *Conclusions and Suggestions for Further Research* | 36 |
|    *The Blancheflour Legend* | 40 |
|    *The Horn Legend* | 41 |
|    *The Squire of Low Degree* | 42 |
| APPENDIX I *List of Middle English Romances* | 45 |
| APPENDIX II *Manuscripts Containing ME Romances* | 64 |
| ENDNOTES | 71 |

## *Acknowledgments*

Like any scholarly author, I have numerous debts, personal as well as intellectual. I have had discussions with many ballad experts over the years, most of them via the Ballad-L mailing list, and I owe them very much. These include the editor and publisher of this series, Ed Cray and Dick Greenhaus. Ed also pushed me on some points about the history of balladry that influenced both the form and the result of the paper. It is conventional to thank editors, but my appreciation is heartfelt. This would be a very different, and lesser, work without his suggestions.

David Engle, Ph. D., has been an unfailing source of encouragement and good advice. Dr. Susan Friedman offered information about romances and corrected the entire book. Norm Cohen, Edie Gale Hays, and others I have forgotten helped with books. Dr. Stephen Carlson and I spent time talking about parsimony and stemmatics. Many years ago, it was Sally Amundson, Ph.D., who—with a casual question about Arthurian history, one of the richest sources of romances—first encouraged me to do research in folklore.

Catie Jo Pidel, who has more than a little of Orpheus's blood in her, knocked loose so many of the key ideas here that I thought of dedicating the book to her. Sarah Cagley gave me a push that led to an important insight into the question of what constitutes a romance.

My parents, Dorothy and Fred Waltz, and Martha Galep and Elizabeth Rosenberg stood by me during the very hard times when this essay was written. Elizabeth also gave me a useful insight into loyalty and "trouthe" and romance which helped me shape my own definition of the terms. I owe her far more than a mere book dedication.

# *Preface*

The metrical romances and the ballads have much in common. The origins of both are lost in history. Both are musical tales telling stories. Both invoke strong emotions, of love and hate and sorrow.

And, often, both involve the same characters. This will be apparent to anyone who studies the ballads of "King Orfeo" and "Hind Horn" and "Blancheflour and Jellyflorice."[1] Examining these three leads to several more. In many of these cases, it is clear beyond a doubt that the romance and the ballad in some way form a pair.

Sometimes ballad and romance cannot even be distinguished, one from the other. The ballad Francis James Child calls "King Edward the Fourth and a Tanner of Tamworth"[2] is known to romance scholars as the "King and the Shepherd" type. Child classes "King Arthur and King Cornwall" as a ballad;[3] Thomas Hahn treats it as a Gawain romance.[4]

And if ballad and romance are linked, which came first? The romances were almost always written down before their ballad equivalents—but this is not proof; and reputable scholars have argued for the priority of the ballads.[5]

This monograph takes one romance-and-ballad pair—the romance known as *Sir Orfeo* and the ballad that Francis James Child titled "King Orfeo"—and looks at the nature of their relationship, trying in the process to establish a methodology for making such comparisons.

Any such discussion must be tentative, because the real question is about the relationship between romances and ballads *as a class*. This is only a start on such a study, with a test of the technique, although it will look at other romance-and-ballad pairs besides the Orpheus complex.

CHAPTER I
# *The Beginnings of Romance*

When William the Conqueror's Normans took over England in 1066, they brought with them more than just a new ruling dynasty. They brought a new language, new customs — and a new literature.

Garnett and Gosse argue "Two characteristics of native [pre-Conquest] English literature will have been remarked, its limited range and its general seriousness."[6] Old English literature featured several genres, from epic (*Beowulf*) to history (Bede, the *Anglo-Saxon Chronicle*) to wisdom literature (Alfred the Great's translation of Boethius) to religious writings (Biblical paraphrases and the homilies of Wulfstan).[7] It featured both poetry and prose, narrative and description. But there is no question but that it was almost all "serious." It's not just that it lacked humor; there is almost nothing designed for simple enjoyment. Even the secular poetry was mostly bleak and rather formulaic.

The Anglo-Norman literature was different. "Storytelling was for the Middle Ages a favorite form of entertainment.... There was a vast appetite for narratives: humorous, sentimental, tragic, pious, and romantic."[8] Perhaps the earliest popular stories were the *chansons de geste*,[9] which like Anglo-Saxon literature were heroic and serious, but that quickly changed.[10] By the twelfth century, poets from Brittany to Provence were producing "romances"— tales of knights and ladies, of love and happiness,[11] of magic and mystery, of separations and unexpected reunions.[12] So popular were they that it has been said that "The romance stands to medieval literature as the novel stands to the literature of the nineteenth and twentieth centuries."[13]

The exact definition of a romance is elusive. A few authors have insisted that it be "romantic"— that is, that it be about love, perhaps specifically "courtly love," or the quest for the unattainable beloved. Another suggestion is "a tale of knightly prowess, usually set in remote times or places and involving elements of the fantastic or supernatural."[14] "Courtesy" is often a key element.[15] Some claim that romances are "inextricably linked with feudalism,"[16] or that their roots are entirely in the Arthurian story.[17]

In the period after the Conquest, "legend and love were the two main themes of the twelfth century literary revolt against earlier religious traditions, and it is not without significance that they were precisely the themes of this new creation, the romance."[18] C. S. Lewis famously argued that the mark of courtly love tales — in which he included the romances — were Humility, Courtesy, Adultery, and the Religion of Love,[19] although the list in Chaucer's description of the Knight seems more fitting: "trouthe and honour, fredom and curteisye."[20] Finally, it is claimed that "the romance moves largely amidst abstractions.... The problems of actual life are carefully avoided; the material treated consists, rather, of the fanciful problems of the courts of love and situations arising out of the new-born chivalry."[21]

And yet, as a group, the romances "are not solely reflections of the psychology of courtly love, nor are they mere embodiments of lax amorosity."[22] Love themes are common but by no means universal. *Athelston*, for instance, has "nothing to do with enchantment or courtly love,"[23] while "Love, which later ages were to associate with romance, plays a very minor part in *Havelock [the Dane]*."[24] "The... *Lai le Freine*... [has] nothing of refined love or *courtoisie*, nothing of chivalry (save for cursory mentions of a tournament that does not take place), nothing of magic or fairie."[25] Even more extremely, *The Tournament of Tottenham* — a tale of a contest of a bunch of peasants to win Tyb the potter's daughter — has little of feudalism in it, and no hint at all of knightly adventures. What's more, a number of romances have almost no female characters — *Gamelyn* and the *Gest of Robyn Hode* are examples of this type.[26]

Furthermore, love "was by no means always viewed as a positive force by Marie [de France] and her contemporaries."[27]

While most romances have happy endings, some do not; there are two romances on the death of Arthur (the stanzaic and alliterative versions of the *Morte Arthure*), and the *Gest of Robyn Hode* also ends with the hero's death. The rule is simply that, if the ending is unhappy, it is for romantic reasons, such as the conflict in the *Morte Arthure* between Lancelot's virtue of love for Guinevere and his virtue of loyalty to Arthur.[28] Nor do the romances always ignore real-world problems; the knight in *The Gest of Robyn Hode* has a debt to an unscrupulous abbot which he cannot pay, and you can almost smell the pig manure exuding from the *Tournament of Tottenham*. And if King Arthur had shown up in *Gamelyn*, the hero most likely would have punched him out.[29]

Magic is common (although there is no sign of it, for example, in the *Gest* or *Gamelyn* or the *Tournament of Tottenham*), but it is not so much witchcraft as we would define it but the hallmark of a world full of brighter colors and sharper shadows than ours: "There is often a sense in the greater romancers that quite ordinary events, ordinary things, have a significance quite beyond themselves, a supernatural significance.... The meaning is not in the marvel but in the experience which it may or may not carry.... Man cannot effectively be a *superman* in a world of bowler-hats, rolled umbrellas, and regular trains to the city."[30]

The romances themselves point out that they treat of many themes; *The Wars of Alexander* says that some hearers of romances have "langing of lufe lays to herken" (that is, they "long to hearken to love lays") while others want to be told "of curtaissy, of knighthode, of craftes or armys" ("of courtesy, of knighthood, of [war]craft or arms"), while still others prefer saints' lives.[31]

The feeling of a romance is often a key: "The sense of beautiful fragility, of something so precious and yet so precarious that it should outweigh our normal feelings of justice and propriety, is part of our response to many romances."[32]

One study defines romance not by its content but by its main character: "If superior in *degree* to other men and to his environment, the hero is the typical hero of *romance*, whose actions are marvelous but who is himself identified as a human being."[33] Another says that romance is "a special experience (or, rather, a set of experiences) of fundamental and continuing importance to Western man. In terms of literature, romance is a genre the conventions of which express these special experiences.... Romance as a genre, a series of related genres, is characterized by conventions, motifs, archetypes which have been created in order to express these experiences in their essential nature."[34]

Often a romance serves to examine ethical or philosophical questions in a way that is difficult to do in ordinary life because ordinary life is so muddy. The medieval romances often feature a sharp divide between Christian and Saracen; Tolkien's modern romance features clear good guys and bad guys.[35]

None of these descriptions really serves to fully define the genre. *Sir Orfeo*, the subject of this study, has fantastic elements and a love theme but no knightly prowess — Orfeo's prowess is musical. *The Gest of Robyn Hode* has no magical elements or love theme, and the only knight has to be rescued by Robin Hood. It is tempting to say that there is no definition — a listener knows a romance upon hearing it.

Or perhaps we should say that a romance has only two requirements: it must feature a hero doing an extraordinary task, and it must be for a worthy cause. It may be Gawain marrying a hag to save Arthur, as in *Sir Gawain and Dame Ragnall* and Chaucer's "Wife of Bath's Tale." It may be Gawain (again) accepting with courage the danger of a fatal blow in *Sir Gawain and the Green Knight*. It may be a lover offering up his life for love (sort of the Official Worthy Cause of the Middle Ages[36]) in *Floris and Blancheflour*. It may be Robin Hood rescuing a knight from poverty in *The Gest of Robyn Hode*. Or it may be Orfeo travelling to the underworld to bring back his beloved. In every instance, it is the story of a hero finding and maintaining what Chaucer calls his "trouthe" — his troth, but far more than simply a vow. It is his pledged word, it is his integrity, it is his loyalty, it is his purpose, his place in the universe, his way of learning to be true to himself.[37] A person without trouthe is not complete; a romance generally serves to restore trouthe in some way. It is "a search for the true self"[38] — although the true self in its context, of society and of love.

Most romances are anonymous,[39] but this is not an absolute necessity; the *lais* of Marie de France are well-known, Chaucer is responsible for several romances, John Gower rewrote some, and Thomas Chestre produced *Sir Launfal* and possibly several other pieces. The authors of the romances studied here are, however, lost in history.

Whatever it is about, the romance must have the power to move us — to pity, to fear, to admiration, to sympathy, to joy. "[T]he essential romance experiences are idealistic."[40] But even this is not enough. It is crucial that there be a genuine possibility of failure — of catastrophic failure. Epic heroes, such as Roland in the *Song of Roland*, know their fate;[41] romantic heroes do not. The ending of a romance must, as J. R. R. Tolkien put it, allow for either *eucatastrophe* or *dyscatastrophe*.[42] Orfeo may rescue Heurodis — or he may fail, and even be taken himself. Sir Gawain may lose his head in the Beheading Game. Floris and Blancheflour, instead of both surviving, may both be killed.

It will take no such broad definition to include *Sir Orfeo*, the subject of this study, in the romances; it is in the style known as the *Breton Lai* (a description that means not "of Brittany" but "of Britain"[43]), it involves a tale of love triumphant, and it takes place largely in Faërie; its place among the romances is undisputed.

The romances proved immensely popular. (Indeed, they are immensely popular today, as works such as Tolkien's *The Lord of the Rings* and Rowling's tales of Harry Potter show; although not metrical, they are just as much romances as *Sir Gawain and the Green Knight* or *Le Morte d'Arthur*.[44] Tolkien in particular was unquestionably imitating the romances.[45]) Shakespeare himself experimented significantly with the form, even though it wasn't one of the standard types of drama in his time.[46]

One estimate places the number of Middle English romances at sixty;[47] Appendix I, by combining many scholars' lists, brings the total even higher. Some are aristocratic, and indeed one scholar has claimed that they existed to reinforce the aristocracy[48] — but most are designed for relatively humble tastes; one author calls most of them *bourgeois*.[49] Carl Lindahl sees some lower-class influences in Chaucer, noting how characters such as the Miller and the Cook demand attention at the expense of characters such as the Franklin, and observes that the low-born Host directs the activities of all.[50]

At least some romances, such as *Havelock the Dane*, are in a small way revolutionary; the composer of that tale "accepts, not birth and power, but work, virtue, and integrity as paramount."[51] It has been said that Havelock is "more plebeian than the majority of ballads."[52] Similarly, the Scottish romance *The Tale of Rauf Coilyear*, although very late by romance standards (c. 1470), is a piece in which "everything is turned upside down in favour of social equality and the common man."[53]

The English romance had a peculiar style, not the same as those in French. Again and again we read of English versions of French tales being shortened, simplified, reshaped. "[T]he English versifier follows his original with fidelity from incident to incident, but in doing so he often speaks from his own English point of view. He adapts his original to his audience by abridgment, by the more frequent use of direct discourse, by the introduction of popular features, occasionally by the addition of a passage of some length, and, less frequently, by the use of another authority."[54]

Although modern romances are often in prose, those in Middle English are poetry. (With, of course, some late exceptions such as Malory.) The poetic forms vary widely. Many, such as *The Wedding of Sir Gawain and Dame Ragnell*, are in "tail rhyme" form,[55] which Chaucer parodied in his "Sir Thopas":[56]

| | |
|---|---|
| Yet listeth, lordes, to my tale | *Yet listen, lords, to my tale,* |
| Murier than the nightyngale, | *Merrier than the nightingale* |
|     For now I wole you rowne |     *For now I will you tell* |
| How sir Thopas, with sydes smale, | *How Sir Thopas, with sides small,* |
| Prikying over hill and dale, | *Hastening over hill and dale,* |
|     Is comen agayn to town.[57] |     *Is come again to town.* |

The tail rhyme format is two long lines followed by a shorter, then another set of two long lines and a shorter, rhyming *aabccb*, with the *b* rhyme often continued in another group to give a twelve-line stanza.

It has been claimed that tail rhyme is the "mark of the popular epic"[58] (as opposed to aristocratic works), but this does not seem to fit surviving compositions. Although tail rhyme is the most common romance format, many others were used. Several texts revive the old Anglo-Saxon alliterative line.[59] A few use composite forms, such as *Sir Gawain and the Green Knight*, with its irregular alliterative stanzas ending with a "bob-and-wheel" of five shorter rhymed lines.[60] Probably the most common form, other than the tail rhyme, is the rhymed couplet, and romances which use this form these include most of the "folkiest," such as *Gamelyn*,[61] *King Horn*,[62] *Floris and Blancheflour*,[63] *The Squire of Low Degree*,[64] the Robin Hood poems, and *Sir Orfeo* itself.

The romances seem to have been designed for public presentation, not private reading; romances, according to Wace, were musical performances, played on vieles, rotas (crwths), harps, and frestels (flutes).[65] The prologue of Chaucer's *Franklin's Tale* further affirms that

> *This olde gentil Britouns in hir dayes*
> *Of diverse aventures maden layes,*
> *Rymeyed in hir firste Briton tonge,*
> *Which layes with hir instrumentz they songe.*[66]

The romances and the ballads have much in common. Both tell stories. Both involve music. Both were generally composed for public performance. The ballads, it's true, involve a much wider range of subjects than the romances (it's hard to imagine an incest romance such as "Lizie Wan" or "Sheathe and Knife"!). But where the themes overlap, there is no inherently obvious characteristic to separate a romance from a ballad. It is a question worth pondering while examining the Orpheus legend.

One of the amazing attributes of romances was their tendency to move from one language to another. Many of the Arthurian tales started with Geoffrey of Monmouth, then moved into the French of Chrétien de Troyes, then were moved into English. The "Breton Lais," the most famous of which were the work of Marie de France, began as Celtic folktales, then were reworked in French, and several of them then came into English. An example is the Lanfaul tale: Marie of France took a folktale and made it into the *Lai de Lanval* which was translated into Middle English as *Sir Landeval* and then turned into *Sir Launfal*.[67]

The tale of Horn, which probably inspired the ballad "Hind Horn," is found in the early English romance *King Horn*, the later *Horn Childe*, and the Anglo-Norman *Horn et Rimenild*.[68] The tale of *Floris and Blancheflour* exists in two French romances and one in English, plus forms from Germany, Iceland, Sweden, Italy, and Spain; there is also a Flemish ballad.[69]

It is so habitual to find a French original for English romances that some have even sought a French original for *Sir Gawain and the Green Knight*,[70] a *tour de force* that patently cannot survive translation. (Witness the fact that it doesn't even translate well from Middle English to Modern English!)

But probably no romance theme had a longer or more complex history than the story of Orpheus, which goes back to classical times and somehow managed to emerge as a fourteenth century English romance and a nineteenth century ballad.

CHAPTER 2

## *The Original Orpheus Myth*

In the classical myth, Orpheus was the son of Calliope the muse. "Such was his power in song, that he could move trees and rocks and tame wild beasts thereby."[71] He could sing more sweetly than even the sirens.[72]

His story seems originally to have been Greek. He is credited with inventing the *kithara*,[73] which is the ancestor (linguistically, at least) of the zither and guitar. His head is said to have continued singing even after he was torn to pieces[74] — or perhaps it was still crying Euridice's name.[75] The constellation Lyra is said to have been made from his instrument.

Although the story is Greek, it was preserved mostly by Latin authors. Three authors — Virgil, Ovid, and Boethius — are believed to have been the sources for the legend as known in Western Europe.

The fullest version of the story is that given at the beginning of Book X of Ovid's *Metamorphoses*. We may summarize it as follows:[76]

Orpheus was about to be married to Euridice, but as Euridice was wandering the meadows with the naiads, she died from the bite of a serpent. Orpheus, having wept bitterly, sought her out in Hades. Having arrived there, he declared before Persephone and Hades that he has come because his love for Euridice was too strong to be borne. He said that he did not ask for Euridice to be immortal, merely to be allowed to be with her for a normal span of years. He declared that, if he could not return to the living world with her, neither did he wish to return alone.

As he sang these words to his harp, even stone-hearted Hades was moved to tears. The Furies themselves briefly gave up their raging. The tortures of Tartarus were halted. The rulers of Hades gave in; Orpheus could lead Euridice, still limping because of her heel, back to the upper world — on condition. He must not look back until they had left Avernus.

"Up the sloping path, through the mute silence they made their way, up the steep dark track, wrapped in impenetrable gloom, till they had almost reached the surface of the earth. Here, anxious in case his wife's strength be failing...

the lover looked behind him, and straightway Euridice slipped back into the depths." He tried to catch her, but there was nothing but air.

Ovid has other tales about Orpheus, including one about how he was murdered, but that is the core story: He lost his wife, went to Hades to find her, won her release, but lost her when he turned back.

Virgil's version is slightly less full but probably more widely available in medieval times. It is found in Book IV of the *Georgics*, lines 453-527:[77]

Orpheus went mad for love of Euridice. She, running heedless from the god Aristeaeus who lusted after her, did not see the deadly serpent hidden in the deep grass by the banks. After she was bitten, the Dryads filled the mountain passes with their cries; even the land wept. Orpheus solaced himself with his music, there by the lonely shore—then entered the lofty doors of Dis, and came to the grove that was dark with terror, and came before the king of terror, whose heart does not soften at human sorrows. [There he played his music] and the phantoms of the darkness themselves came to hear the surprising sound. Even through the dark mires they came, spellbound. The Furies, Cerberus—the walls and torture-chambers themselves were rapt, and the lords of the land gave him his request.

Upward he retraced his steps. "He had escaped every mischance, and the regained Eurydice was nearing the upper world, following behind—for that condition had Proserpine ordained—when a sudden frenzy seized Orpheus, unwary in his love." "Surely it would be forgiven—if Hell knew forgiveness." But the agreement was broken, and the bells of Avernus tolled, and she was torn away, crying, "What madness has ruined myself and thee." Faintly she bade farewell as she was carried away, and he could not again follow, for the guardians of the gate would not let him pass.

The tellings are very different, but the heart of the story is the same: Euridice died from the bite of a snake. Orpheus entered into Hell to bring her back. His music moved even the stone-hearted Hades himself. Orpheus might bring her back to life—if he never looked back until they were back in the upper world. But, at the last moment, he turned around, and Euridice was lost to him forever.

A third Latin telling is that of Boethius's *Consolation of Philosophy*.[78] This certainly continued to be known, since Alfred the Great translated it into Old English (while tacking on a moralizing conclusion in which Orpheus's looking back is equivalent to moral backsliding),[79] but it almost certainly did not have the level of influence of the great earlier writers. As the Orpheus legend entered the Middle Ages, it was the versions of Ovid ("whose influence was everywhere visible" in the period when the romances became popular[80]) and Virgil which most people knew.

The tale of Orpheus and Euridice has been called "the most famous of romantic myths."[81] Little wonder it became a romance!

## CHAPTER 3
## *The Romance* Sir Orfeo

The history of the Orpheus legend after the time of Boethius is unknown to us. For more than five hundred years after his time, we have no tellings of the legend, other than Alfred's translation of Boethius, until the tale next manifests itself in the thirteenth or fourteenth century in the Middle English romance *Sir Orfeo*. But it clearly was remembered.

Robert Henryson published a poem "Orpheus and Euridice" in the sixteenth century based primarily on Boethius.[82] It is widely believed that there must have been a French romance of Orpheo: "*Sir Orfeo* is probably an adaption of a French Breton lay. No French version survives, but there are references in French romances to a musical 'Lai d'Orphey.'"[83]

There is a version of the Orpheus legend in Lefèvre's *Recueil des Hystoires Troyennes* which has some similarities to *Sir Orfeo* in that the otherworld king releases Euridice in response to a rash promise,[84] but this canot be a source for *Sir Orfeo*, because Lefèvre lived in the fifteenth century—and his version of the story refers to Pluto, not the King of Faërie.[85] At most it might testify to the contents of the French source for *Sir Orfeo*.

The loss of the French, or Breton, or Latin original is particularly to be regretted because we know that there were two English romances about the Orpheus legend, *Sir Orfeo* and *Orpheus, King of Portugal*.[86] Lyle is convinced that the latter is the source of the ballad "King Orfeo." But most of it has been lost. The surviving text is only about 150 lines—too little to tell us much. Even if *Sir Orfeo* is based on an original in a different language, it is likely that it has been reworked.

Most translation romances are rather stale. *Sir Orfeo*, by consensus, is not. "Chaucer's 'Wife of Bath's Tale' and 'Franklin's Tale' aside, it stands as the all-around success among English poems classed as Breton *lais*."[87] Some regard it as one of Chaucer's stylistic inspirations.[88] *Orfeo* may be derivative, but it is not a simple translation. It gives every sign of having been elaborated. Indeed, based on the story as it now stands, it could be the elaboration of a ballad.

Somewhere in the evolution from literary legend to romance, the tale has been greatly changed. Classical stories retold for in the Middle Ages generally took on the trappings of medieval life,[89] and *Sir Orfeo* is no exception. "The Greek myth is almost lost in a tale of fairyland, the earliest English romance of the kind."[90] "[T]he story has been reinterpreted as a Celtic folk-tale."[91] Orpheus the minstrel becomes Orfeo the aristocrat who just happens to be a musician. Euridice is Heurodis, and she is taken from the world after sleeping beneath an enchanted tree, not due to snakebite.

The other-world setting is Faërie, not Hades. This is a major change, and not just in terms of the religion of the hearers. Hades is dark and gloomy, but "*Faerie* contains many things besides elves and fays... it holds the sea, the sun, the moon, the sky; and the earth, and all things that are in it: tree and bird, water and stone, wine and bread, and ourselves, mortal men, when we are enchanted."[92] It is not a land where dark rules everything, and where even the bitter air and foul water are oppressive. One can visit Faerie and return, as Thomas of Ercildoune supposedly did.[93] Nor, it appears, is a visit to Faerie inherently hazardous to the soul.[94] The change of place allows for a happy ending.

Indirectly, it allows another, more subtle change which strengthens the romantic aspect of the tale. In the classical legend, Orpheus heads directly for Hades to win back his wife. But in *Sir Orfeo*, Orfeo wanders for ten years; in "King Orfeo," for seven. What was, in the classical legend, purely a tale of love becomes, in a great measure, a tale of constancy and loyalty. Loyalty is one of the great romantic virtues;[95] it is a change that gives the romance a very different feel.

Stories much like that of Orfeo were told in Celtic legend. Walter Map reported, a knight of Lesser Brittany lost his wife, and went on mourning for her long after her death. At last he found her by night in a great company of women in a valley surrounded by desert. Seeing her alive again he could not believe his eyes, and wondered what the fairies could be doing. But he snatched her away and enjoyed a union with her for many years."[96]

Yet "neither classical nor Celtic legends account entirely for the English *Sir Orfeo.*"[97] There are a number of deft little touches which make the result very English. A feeble attempt is made in *Sir Orfeo* to translate the story from Greece to Winchester;[98] this is surely the work of the English poet, not any French versifier! There is, it is true, an English romance (*Guy of Warwick*) which partially parallels the story of the rescue of Heurodis.⁹⁹ The original motivation of the Orpheus legend is still there; the hero is still a musician who leaves the bounds of the world to rescue his lost love. But the rest is all changed.

There are three surviving copies of *Sir Orfeo*. The earliest is from the famous Auchinleck manuscript of the fourteenth century,¹⁰⁰ which is the basis for almost every edition now in print.¹⁰¹ The other two are both fifteenth century, Bodleian MS. Ashmole 61 (another very important source) and British Library MS. Harley 3810.¹⁰² These two both add a several-dozen-line preface describing the nature of a romance lacking from the Auchinleck copy (which is missing a page); this preface is usually included with *Sir Orfeo* even though it is also found in, and may derive from, another romance, the *Lay le Friene*.

We may summarize the plot of *Sir Orfeo* as follows, with references to the relevant lines in []:

Orfeo is a king [line 25] and a harper [34] whose kingdom is based in Winchester [49]. His queen, Heurodis [52], goes to a garden [64] and goes mad [78] after sleeping beneath a tree. Orfeo is not present, but arrives soon after Heurodis has her fit [97]. Asked why she has behaved as she has, Heurodis reports that a king with a hundred knights told her that she will come with him [135-174]. Orfeo assembles a guard for her [181-185], but she vanishes from their midst [191]. Orfeo appoints a steward to keep his kingdom so he can go hunt her [203]. He lives in the wild [228], going barefoot and letting his hair and beard grow long, but still he carries his harp [231]. He is ten years in the wild [265], hiding his harp in a tree when it rains [270]. At last he sees the King of Faërie with a thousand knights [290]. At other times, he sees fine ladies [300]. Finally he sees Heurodis in the fey company [320]. Grieving [330], he sets out to follow the company [340]. The ladies enter Faërie by a rock, and he follows. He comes to the astounding castle of the King [358], enters as a wandering minstrel [382], and sees more wondrous sights before reaching the King's hall [410]. The king speaks sternly of his rashness, but allows him to play [430]. (There is no description of the type of music Orfeo played, except that it is on the harp [440-445]). The King of Faërie shows no sign of knowing of Orfeo's relationship with Heurodis [457], but the King grants Orfeo a wish in return for his playing [450]. Orfeo asks for Heurodis [455]. The king says Orfeo and Heurodis are no match, but — reminded of his promise — grants the boon [469]. They return without incident to the ordinary world [475]. Orfeo comes to his kingdom still in beggar's garb [500], and asks help of his steward [510]. The steward grants it to honor Orfeo's memory [515]. Orfeo plays very well [525]—and the steward recognizes Orfeo's harp. He asks how he found it [530]. Orfeo tells of finding it by the body of a man torn by lions [538] ten years previously. The steward mourns [542], and Orfeo, knowing that the man has been faithful, tells his tale [553]. The steward and lords cast themselves at Orfeo's feet [575]. Orfeo is re-crowned [592]; the singer concludes with good wishes to all.

A full prose modernization of the text follows. Figures in [brackets] again refer to line numbers in the original, based on the edition of Sisam.[103] The poetic form of the original will doubtless often be obvious—after all, this is a "translation" from English into English! But the emphasis is on retaining the meaning of the original; the translation is in prose because rhyme and meter have been sacrificed to accuracy in meaning. Major variants in the text, or places where the meaning is unclear or requires amplification, are shown in the notes.

The first two dozen lines of the poem, shown in *italics*, are not in the Auchinleck manuscript; they are a reconstruction based on the other two manuscripts and other sources. They are included even though the present author is far from sure they are part of the original poem.

# Sir Orfeo

[1] *We often read, and find written—as scribes know so well—that songs played with the harp are based on marvelous things. Some tell of war,[104] and some of woe; some tell of joy and mirth. Some tell of treachery, and some of guile; some of things that happened long ago. Some tell of bawdry and of ribaldry—[10] and some are about Faërie.[105] But of all the things that men may see, the most of them are about love.*

*In Britain these songs are written—they were first found there and then sent forth. Tales of things in bygone days—of them the British made their lays. When kings might hear from anywhere of any marvels, they took their harps with glee[106] and joy, and made their songs and gave them names.[107] [20] Of the adventures that took place in times past, I can tell some, but not all. So listen, lordlings with hearts true, and I will tell you of Sir Orfeo.*

[25] Orfeo was a king, in England a high lord, a stalwart man, and hardy too, generous and courteous as well. His father was descended from King Pluto [30] and his mother from King Juno—who once were said to be gods, because of the adventures that they did and told.

[33][108] *Orfeo most of anything loved the glee of harping; every harper that came him before was certain to have great honor. He himself loved to harp, and put his fine wits to that end. He learned so well, [40] a better harper could not be found anywhere. In the world was never a man born that would be placed ahead of Orfeo; anyone who might hear harping would think that he were in one of the joys of Paradise—such joy and melody was in his harping!*

[47] This king sojourned in Thrace,[109] that was a city of strong defenses—for Winchester, without doubt, [50] was called Thrace back then.

[51] The king had a wonderful queen who was known as Dame Herodis,[110] the fairest lady, you may know, ever formed of flesh and bone, so full of love and goodness that none could tell her beauty.

[57] It happened at the beginning of May, when merry and hot is the day, and the winter showers have gone away, [60] and every field is full of flowers, and blossoms are bright on every bough, and all things wax merry enough, that this queen, Dame Herodis, took two wonderful maids and went in the

morning to play by an orchard side — to see the flowers spread and spring and to hear the birds sing.

[69] All three of them sat down [70] under a grafted[111] tree, and soon after this fair queen fell asleep upon the green. The two maids did not dare awaken her, but let her lie and take her rest. So she slept until after noon; morning was past and done. But as soon as she woke up, she cried out and began to shriek horribly. She wrung her hands and her feet, [80] and scratched her face till the blood ran red; her fine rich robe she tore to shreds. Her wits were stolen away! The two maids standing by dared not stay with her any longer. Both ran at once to the palace, and told both squire and knight that their queen had gone mad, and bade them go and hold her. Knights and ladies both ran — [90] sixty damsels and more!

[91] They hurried to the orchard where the queen was, and took her up in their arms. At last they brought her to bed, and held her there very securely. But she cried out in the same way again and again, and tried to be up and away.

[97] When Orfeo heard the news, it was the worst he had ever had. He arrived with ten knights [100] at the chamber, and came where the queen was, and looked, and said piteously, "O love of my life, what is wrong, that you who were always so still now cry out so very shrill? Your body, that was so beautifully white, now is all torn by your own nails![112] Your hue, that was so red, now is as wan as if you were dead, and also your fingers so small [110] are both bloody and pale. Alas! Your two lovely eyes look at me as a man looks at his foe. Ah, lady, I beg you, mercy! Let your rueful cries end; tell me what troubles you, and how, and whatever thing could help you now."

[117] Then finally she lay still, and began to weep very hard, and said to the king, [120] "Alas, my lord, Sir Orfeo! Never, since we were first together, have we ever been angry with each other. Always I have loved you as my life — and you me. But now we must be separated; do your best, for I must go."

[127] "Alas!" said he, "I am forlorn! Where will you go, and to whom? Where you go, I will go with you, [130] and where I go, you shall go with me."[113] "Nay, nay, sir, that cannot be! Let me tell you the whole story. As I lay down this morning, and slept under our orchard, there came to me two fair knights, armed well and properly, who bid me come quickly and speak with their lord the king. I answered with bold words, [140] 'You dare not, nor do I want to.' They spurred away, riding hard. Then came their king,[114] also in haste, with a hundred knights and more, and a hundred damsels also. All were

19

on snow-white steeds, their clothes white as milk. I never saw such a sight before—such fine, fair creatures they were. The king had a crown on his head [150] that was not of silver or red gold, but it was all of a precious stone; as bright as the sun it shone. And as soon as he came to me, with or against my wishes, he took me and made me ride upon a palfrey by his side. He took me to his palace, finely adorned in every way, and showed me castles and towers, [160] rivers, forests, glades with flowers, and his rich steeds—every one! And then he brought me home again, into our own orchard, and then he said to me, 'Take heed, dame, that tomorrow you be right here under this grafted tree. Then you shall with us go, and live with us forevermore. And if you make trouble for us, [170] wherever you be—we will fetch you! And tear you limb from limb, and nothing will be able to help. And even after you are so torn, even then you will be taken away.'"

[175] When King Orfeo heard the news, "Oh, woe," he cried. "Alas, alas! I would sooner lose my life than thus to lose the queen, my wife!" He asked advice of every man, [180] but no man can help him at all.

[181] When the next morning came, Orfeo took his arms, and a thousand knights with him—each one armed, stout and grim. He went with the queen straight to that grafted tree. They made a schiltrom[115] on each side, and said that they would abide there, and all of them die there, [190] before the queen should be taken from them. And yet, right from their midst, the queen was snatched away—taken by enchantment. No one knew where she was gone.

[195] And oh, was there an outcry, weeping and wailing, then! The king went to his chamber, and often swooned on the stone floor, and made such grief and moan that his life was almost spent. [200] But there was no change. He called together his barons, earls, and lords of renown. And when they all were come, he said, "Lords, before you here, I ordain my high steward to rule my kingdom from now on. He shall stand in my place to keep all my lands. For now that I have lost my queen, [210] the fairest lady that ever was born, never again will I see any woman. Into the wilderness I shall go, and live there forevermore, with the wild beasts in the hoary woods. And when you learn that I am dead, then make yourselves a parliament and choose yourself a new king.[116] Now do your best with all my holdings."

[219] Then there was weeping in the hall, [220] and a great cry among all of them. Neither old nor young could speak a word because of their weeping.

All together they knelt down, and begged him, if it would consent, that he not go from them.

[226] "Give it up!" he said. "It shall be so." All his kingdom he forsook; he took nothing but a pilgrim's garment. He had no tunic or hood, [230] nor shirt, nor any other possessions—except his harp; at least he took that! He went barefoot out the gate; no man might go with him. Oh woe! So much weeping and wailing, when he who had been a crowned king went so poorly out of town! Into the wilderness he went, through wood and over heath. He found nothing to give him ease, [240] but ever he lived in great malaise. He who had worn striped and grey furs, who had slept in purple linen, now lay on the hard heath, wrapped in leaves and grass. He who had had castles and towers, river, forest, glades with flowers—now, when it starts to snow and frost, this king has to make his bed in moss. He who had had wonderful knights [250] kneeling before him, and ladies, now sees nothing that pleases him, but wild worms glide by him. He that had had plenty of meat and drink, and it dainty, now had to dig and grub all day must merely to find his fill of roots. In summer he lived by wild fruit and poor berries. In winter he could find nothing [260] but roots, grasses, and bark. His whole body dwindled away from the hardship, and was chapped all over. Lord! who may tell the sorrow the king suffered for ten years and more? The hair of his beard, black and rough, grew all the way to his belt.[117] His harp, in which was all his glee, he hid in a hollow tree, and when the weather was clear and bright, [270] then he took the harp to him, and harped at his own desire. In all the wood the sound rang forth, so that all the wild animals that were there gathered about him in joy, and all the birds that were there came and sat, each on a briar, to hear his fine harping—so much melody was therein! And when he would stop his harping, [280] no beast would remain by him.

[281] Often, on hot mornings, he would see near him the king of Faërie with his host, come to hunt all about, with faint cries and blowing of horns, and hounds, too, barking with him. But they never took any beasts, nor could he ever tell where they came from. At other times he might see [290] as great a host go by him, well-equipped, a thousand knights, each properly armed, with faces determined and fierce, and many banners unfurled, and each holding his drawn sword—but he never knew where they wished to go.

[297] At other times, he saw something else: knights and ladies come dancing, in fine clothing, gracefully—[300] fine movements, and soft. They had ta-

bors and trumpets with them, and all sorts of minstrelsy. And then, one day, he saw sixty ladies on horses riding by him. They were gentle and jolly as a bird on a green limb, and not one man with them. Each one bore a falcon on her hand; each rode by the river to hawk. They found an abundance of game—[310] mallards, herons, and cormorants. The birds of the water arose; the falcons marked them well. Each falcon slew its prey. Orfeo saw that, and laughed. "By my faith!" he said, "There is fair game. I shall go there, by God's name. I want to see that sort of work!" He arose and went toward them. He came to a lady, [320] and saw her, and saw that it was his own queen, Dame Herodis. He was thrilled to see her, and she him—but neither spoke a word to the other. With sorrow she sighed to see him, who had been so rich, so high; the tears fell from her eyes. The other ladies saw this, and made her ride away—[330] she must no longer stay with him.

[331] "Alas!" said he, "Now woe is me. Why will not death slay me now? Alas, wretched me, that I may not die after this sight. Alas! My life lasts too long, when I dare not be with my wife! Nor she to me [dared] to speak one word. Alas! Why will my heart not break? By my faith!" he said, "Whatever may happen, [340] wherever this lady ride, I shall go the same way, caring neither for life nor death."

[343] His pilgrim's garment he speedily put on, and hung his harp upon his back; he was determined to be on his way. Neither stock nor stone slowed him. Right into a rock[118] the ladies rode, and he followed without hesitation.

[349] When he went into the rock, [350] he travelled another three miles, and came to a fair country, as bright as the sun on a summer day, smooth and level and covered with green. There wasn't a hill or dale to be seen. In the middle of the land he saw a castle, rich and royal and wonderfully high. All the outermost walls were clear and shone like crystal. It was guarded by a hundred towers, [360] extraordinary, with strong battlements. The buttresses that rose from the ditch were made of red gold. The arches were decorated with all sorts of enamel. It was full of spacious apartments made of precious stones. Even the worst pillar was all of burnished gold. The entire land was always lit, [370] for when it was time for dark and night, the rich stones poured out light, as bright as the sun's light at noon. No one can tell, or even think, the rich work that had been wrought there. It all made him think that this was the proud court of Paradise.

[377] In this castle the ladies alighted; he would follow after if he could. Orfeo knocked at the gate; [380] the porter was ready, and asked what he wanted. "By my faith!" he said, "Look, I am a minstrel. I would solace your lord with my glee, if this be his sweet will." The porter at once opened the gate and let him go into the castle.

[387] Then he could see all about, confined within the wall, all sorts of folks that had been taken there, [390] and were thought dead, but were not. Some stood without heads, and some had no arms, and some had wounds through the body, and some were mad and bound. Some sat armed on horses; some had been strangled as they ate. Some had been drowned in water; some had been devoured by fire. Wives lay there on childbed, [400] some dead and some gone mad, and a great many lay there, asleep as if it were morning. Thus each was taken in this world, and with the faërie-power were brought there. There he saw his own wife, Dame Herodis, the love of his life, asleep beneath a grafted tree — by her clothes he knew it was her.

[409] When he had witnessed all these marvels, [410] he went into the king's hall. There he saw a seemly sight, a covered seat beautiful and bright, in which the master king sat, and his queen, fair and sweet. Their crowns and clothes shone so bright that he could hardly look at them. When he had seen all this, he knelt down before the king, "Oh lord, if be your will, [420] my minstrelsy you shall hear." The king answered, "What man are you, who comes hither now? Neither I nor anyone with me sent for you. Since I began to reign here, I never found so foolhardy a man as to dare to come hither to us, unless I wanted to summon him."

[429] "Lord," he said, "know full well: [430] I am nothing but a poor minstrel. And, sire, it is our manner to seek many a lord's house. Even when we are not welcome, still we must offer up our glee." Before the king he sat down and took his harp so merry of sound, and tuned his harp, as he was well able to do, and began to play blissful notes there. All those who were in the palace [440] came out to hear him, sitting down at his feet, they thought his melody so sweet.

[443] The king hearkened and sat full still; he had a good will to hear the glee. Great pleasure he took when he heard the glee, as did the queen.

[447] When [Orfeo] had finished his harping, the king said to him, "Minstrel, I liked this glee very much. [450] Now ask whatever you want of me; great reward I will pay you. Speak, so that you may find this out." "Sire," he

said, "I beseech you that you would give to me that very lady, fair of skin, who sleeps under the grafted tree."

[457] "No," said the king, "Not a chance! A sorry couple you would be! For you are lean, rough, and black, [460] and she is lovely, without defect. A loathly thing it were, therefore, to send her in your company!"

[463] "Oh, sire," he answered, "Gentle king, yet were it a still fouler thing to hear a lie come from your mouth. So, sir, as you said just now, what I asked, I should have — and you should hold to your word."

[469] The king said, "Since it is so, [470] take her by the hand, and go — I hope that you shall be happy with her."[119]

[472] He knelt down, and quickly thanked [the King]. His wife he took by the hand, and swiftly made his way out of that land; he took his way out of that country, leaving by the same way he had come. He took the long way; back to Winchester[120] he came, that had been his own city. [480] But no one knew that it was he. He dared not go farther than the town's limits, lest he be recognized. But he took his lodging in a beggar's small space, for himself and for his wife, as a minstrel of a poor life. He asked tidings of the land, and who held the kingdom in his hand. The poor beggar in his cottage [490] told him every bit: how the queen was stolen away, ten years gone, by fairies; and how the king went into exile, but no one knew in which land; and how the steward held the land; many other things he told.

[497] The next day, around noon, [Orfeo] made his wife stay there. He borrowed the beggar's clothes,[121] [500] and hung his harp upon his back, and went into the city, so that men might look and see him. Earls and barons bold, townsfolk and ladies saw him. "Look!" they said, "Such a man! See how long his hair is! Look! His beard hangs to his knee! He is twisted like a tree!" And, as he went down the street, [510] he met his steward. And loudly he cried out to him, "Sir Steward!" he said, "Mercy! I am a harper from heathen lands. Help me now in this distress!" The steward said, "Come with me, come. Of what I have, you shall have some. Every good harper is welcome to me, for the love of my lord, Sir Orfeo."

[519] In the castle the steward sat at dinner, [520] and many lords sat by him; there were trumpeters and tabor players, many harpers, and crwth-players. They all made much melody. And Orfeo sat still in the hall, and listened, and when all was quiet, he took his harp and tuned it clearly. He harped the most blissful notes than ever any man heard with his ear. Every man liked his

glee very well. [530] The steward watched and began to see, and knew the harp at once. "Minstrel!" he said, "If you wish to do well, from where did you get this harp, and how? I pray that you tell me now." "Lord," he said, "in a strange land, through a wilderness as I traveled, there I found in a dale a man torn to pieces by lions, his body fretted by wolves. [540] By him I found this harp. It was fully ten years ago."

[542] "Oh," said the steward, "Now woe is me. That was my lord, Sir Orfeo! Alas, wretch, what shall I do, I who have lost such a lord? Oh, woe that I was born! That he suffered so hard a fate, and was marked out for such a vile death!" He fell to the ground in a swoon. [550] His barons took him up at that time, and told him how things pass: "There is no cure for a man's death."

[553] King Orfeo after that knew well that his steward was a true man, and loved him as he ought to do. He stood up, and said, "Look, steward, hearken now this thing: If I were Orfeo the king, and had suffered years ago [560] much sorrow in the wilderness, and had won my queen away from the land of Faërie, and had brought the gracious lady right to the town's limits, and lodged her with a beggar, and were myself come hither, in poverty, to you—by this means to test your good will, and found you thus true, [570] you should never rue it. Surely, for love or fear, you should be king after my day. And if you had rejoiced to hear of my death, you should have been cast aside just as swiftly."

[575] Then all who sat there realized that it was King Orfeo. And the steward knew him well—he threw aside the table-board and fell down at his feet. [580] So did every lord sitting there, and all declared with one voice, "You are our lord, sire, and our king!" Glad they were to see him alive; to his chamber they led him at once, and bathed him, and shaved his beard, and attired him to look like a king, and then, with a great procession, they brought the queen into the town with all sorts of minstrelsy. [590] Lord! There was great melody. For joy they wept with their eyes to see them come home sound.

[592] Now King Orfeo is newly crowned, and his queen, Dame Herodis. They lived long afterward, and then the steward was king.

[597] Harpers in Britain after that heard how this marvel began, and made thereof a lay of good delight, [600] and named it after the king. That lay is called "Orfeo"; the lay is good; the note is sweet. Thus Sir Orfeo came out of his care. God grant us well to fare.[122]

## CHAPTER 4
## *The Ballad "King Orfeo"*

There are four known versions of the ballad of the musician-king and the stolen queen. The full list of known versions is as follows:

I. Collected by Biot Edmonston from Andrew Coutts. Printed in *Leisure Hour*, 1880. 17 stanzas, with known defects after stanzas 4 and 8.[123] This was the only version known to Child, who was responsible for giving it the name "King Orfeo."

II. Collected by Francis M. Collinson from Kitty Anderson, Shetland 12 stanzas, with tune. Text, tune in Bronson IV, pp. 455–456.

III. Source unknown. From Shetland. Collected by Bruce Sutherland, 1865. 21 stanzas. Originally printed in *The Shetland News*, August 25, 1894.[124]

IV. Collected by Patrick Shuldham-Shaw from John Stickle, Lerwick, Shetland, 1947. 4 stanzas, with tune. Text, Tune in Bronson I, p. 275.

Version IV is only a fragment but has a solid tune.

Version II is an oddity. The tune is effectively identical to IV, but the words are almost verbatim from I, with a few verses lost. There is good reason to believe it has been influenced by print.

That means that we have one authentic tune (IV) and two significant texts (I and III). These two texts have some overlap, and a few places where they clearly derive from the same original but have diverged since. Both have clearly suffered losses of text—but *different* losses. Neither one really tells a complete story, but by conflating them, we get a fairly substantial text. There may still be material missing, but we are left with a workable ballad.

There has been at least one previous attempt to combine the two texts, by Emily Lyle,[125] but she simply sets the two versions side by side. This is good if one wishes to see how the two versions differ, but it doesn't really show us the likely content of the combined ballad. For our comparison, we need to have that.

A reconstruction follows. No attempt has been made to ensure entire consistency in spelling or orthography; any line may be taken from any version, or patched slightly (for spelling; there are no changes in meaning). The text below lists Child's verse numbers (for verses found in Child), then gives the text of the line. In the right-hand margin is a list of the versions which contain it, and their stanza numbers. For instance, the first line reads

1    Der lived a king inta da aste, I.1a, II.1a

The numeral "1" at left means that it is the first line of Child's first verse. The text of that line is "Der lived a king inta da aste." The notation at right means that this text, or something very like it, is found in versions I.1a, and II.1a. In other words, a text very like this is found in verse one, line a, of version I (Child's/Edmonston's) and in verse one, line a, of version II (Anderson's).

The third stanza of the combined version begins

2    Dis king he has a-huntin' gaen, I.2a, II.2a, (III.2a)

This means that, although it is the third stanza of the combined text, it is the first line of Child's *second* verse. This is found in versions I.2a, II.2a, and (III.2a). In other words, a text very like this is found in verse two, line a, of version I (Child's/Edmonston's), in verse two, line a, of version II (Anderson's), and in verse two, line A, of version III (Sutherland's). But the text of version III is significantly different—"One day the king a hunting went." This is demonstrated by the format (III.2a), indicating that the verse in version III, while having the same general intent, uses different words. A typical instance where the two texts diverge is the lady's name: "Isabel" in I/II, "Lisa Bell" in III.[126] This is important because it indicates that the two versions aren't derived from the same immediate original with some loss of text. There has been at least some evolution along the way (even if, as is possible, it consists of little more than the duplication of stanzas 7 and 12 in version I and the change in the lady's name). A few words are glossed below the text; these are marked *. Brackets [] mark places where it strongly appears something has been lost; [***] are lacunae in noted in Child's text, while [] are losses that I have conjectured.

| VS# | TEXT | IN VERSIONS |
|---|---|---|
| 1 | Der lived a king inta da aste, | I.1a, II.1a, (III.1a) |
| | *Scowan ürla grün* | cho_a, (II.cho_a), III.cho_a, IV.cho_a |
| | Der lived a lady in da wast. | I.1b, II.1b |
| | *Whar giorten han grün oarlac.* | I.cho_b, (II.cho_b), (III.cho_b), (IV.cho_b) |
| 1A | There lived a lady in yon Haa, | III.1a |
| | Her name was lady Lisa Bell. | III.1b |
| 2 | Dis king he has a-huntin' gaen, | I.2a, II.2a, (III.2a) |
| | He's left his Lady Isabel alane. | I.2b, II.2b |
| 2A | [ | ] |
| | They wounded the Lady to the heart. | III.2b |
| 2B | So when the King came home at noon | III.4a |
| | He asked for Lady Lisa Bell. | III.4b |
| 3 | "Oh I wis ye'd never gaen away, | I.3a, II.3a |
| | For at your hame is dule* an wae. | I.3b, II.3b |
| 3A | His nobles unto him did say, | III.5a |
| | My lady was wounded, but now is dead. | III.5b |
| 4 | "For da king o Ferrie* wi' his daert, | I.4a, II.4a, III.3a |
| | Has pierced your lady to da hert." | I.4b, II.4b, III.3b |
| 4A | Now they have taen* her life fra me, | III.6a |
| | But her corps they's never hae. | III.6b |
| 4B | Now he have called his nobles aa, | III.7a |
| | To waltz her corps into the Haa. | III.7b |
| 4C | But when the Lords was fa'en* asleep, | III.8a |
| | Her corps out of the house did sweep. | III.8b |
| 4D | Now he's way to the wood, wood* were, | III.9a |
| | And there he's to sit till grown o'er we hair. | III.9b |
| 4E | He had not sitten seven long years, | III.10a |
| | Till a company to him drew near. | III.10b |

| | | |
|---|---|---|
| 4F | Some did ride and some did ging,* | III.11a |
| | He saw his Lady them among. | III.11b |
| 4G | There stood a Haa upon yon hill, | III.12a |
| | There went aa the Ladie's tilt.* | III.12b |
| | [***] | |
| 5 | And aifter dem the king has gaen, | I.5a, II.5a, (III.13.a) |
| | But whan he cam it was a grey stane.* | I.5b, II.5b, III.13.b |
| 6 | Dan he took oot his pipes ta play, | I.6a, II.6a, III.14b |
| | Bit sair his hert wi' dule an wae.* | I.6b, II.6b, III.14a |
| 7 | And first he played da notes o noy,* | I.7a, II.7a, III.15a |
| | An dan he played da notes o joy. | I.7b, II.7b, III.15.b |
| 8 | An dan he played da gude gabber* reel | I.8a, III.16.a |
| | Dat meicht* ha made a sick hert hale. | I.8b, III.16.b |
| 9 | "Noo come ye in into oor ha', | I.9a, IV.1a, (III.17.a) |
| | "An come ye in among wis a'." | I.9b, (III.17.b) |
| 10 | Now he's gaen in inta der ha', | I.10a, II.8a, (IV.1b, 2a, 2b) |
| | An he's gaen in among dem a'. | I.10b, II.8b, (IV.1b, 2a, 2b) |
| 11 | Dan he took oot his pipes to play, | I.11a, II.9a |
| | Bit sair* his hert wi dule* and wae. | I.11b, II.9b |
| 12 | An first he played da notes o noy,* | I.12a, IV.3a |
| | An dan he played da notes o joy. | I.12b, IV.3b |
| 13 | An dan he played da gude gabber* reel | I.13a, IV.4a |
| | Dat meicht* ha made a sick hert hale. | I.13b, IV.4b |
| 14 | "Noo tell to us what ye will hae:* | I.14a, II.10a, (III.18.a) |
| | What sall* we gie* you for your play?" | I.14b, II.10b, III.18.b |
| 15 | "What I will hae,* I will ye tell | I.15a, II.11a, III.19.a |
| | An dat's me Lady Isabel." | I.15b, II.11b. III.19.b |
| 15A | Thy sister's son, that unworthy thing | III.20.a |
| | To-morrow [w]as to be crowned king | III.20.b |

| | | |
|---|---|---|
| 16 | "Yees tak your lady, an yees gang hame, | I.16a, II,12a, III.21.a |
| | An yees be king ower a' your ain."* | I.16b, II.12b, III.21.b |
| 17 | He's taen his lady, an he's gaen hame | I.17a |
| | An noo he's a king ower a' his ain.* | I.17b |

**Glossary:**
ain: own
dule: grief, sadness
fa'en: fallen
Ferrie: Faërie, the realm of enchantment; see note 105
gabber reel: a dance tune, according to most sources[127]
gie: give
ging: go on foot
meicht: might
noy: sorrow. I.e. "notes o noy" = "sad notes"
sair: sore
sall: shall
stane: stone. I.e. "whan he cam it was a grey stane," = "when he came [to the entrance to Faerie] it was a grey stone.
taen: taken
wood: i.e. wud(e), mad, so "wood were" = "out of his mind."
tilt: company
wae: woe

There are several noteworthy points about this text. First, *the king is never named.* None of the texts identifies him. The name "King Orfeo" was supplied by Child; it does not belong with the known versions. Second, the queen is "Isabel" or "Lisa Bell"—names which are clearly related to each other but not to "Euridice." Third, the king's instrument is the pipes, not the harp or lyre. These are points to which we shall return.

## CHAPTER 5
## *Comparing the Versions*

As we have seen, the relationship between ballads and romances is often unclear. Holger Olof Nygard once asked, "Were the ballads as a genre the work of professional ballad-makers or minstrels, or were they as a class the fortuitous, natural growth of a poetic mode of expression amongst unsophisticated people loosely termed the folk? That the minstrels made some ballads and that they were purveyors of many no one has disputed or will dispute. But what of the origins? Were they by way of the romances or not?"[128]

Most comparisons of *Sir Orfeo* to "King Orfeo" have been casual — typically, they assume that *Sir Orfeo* is older than the ballad because the earliest copies are older, and because it is older, it follows that it is the source of "King Orfeo." It also sometimes assumed that, because the romances appear "superior" to the ballads in terms of style or "elevation," that the romances must therefore be earlier.[129]

The first of these points, about the age of the copies, is strong, but it is not proof. The second point, that the older text must be the source, is weaker still. The third point is no more than an assumption. Yet it is possible, in this case at least, to offer clear proof.

That proof lies in the techniques of classical textual criticism (which Child knew though his followers often do not) and biological stemmatics (which even Child did not know). The ultimate version of this is the biological method known as "cladistics," used determine how closely related various species are. What cladistics does is, in effect, compare information about two or more things (which can be anything from DNA to readings of an old manuscript) and determine which traits go back to an ancestor and which don't.[130] The techniques of cladistics have since been applied, for example, to determine the family tree of manuscripts of Chaucer, and have more recently been applied to manuscripts of the Bible.[131] Cladistics is definitely overkill for this task, but the basic method of "parsimony"[132] can readily be applied.

To borrow a phrase from economist Paul Krugman, this gets "wonkish."

What we do, in this case, is simply compare the three versions of the tale we have, the original legend of Ovid and Virgil, the form found in *Sir Orfeo*, and the form found in "King Orfeo." If we were comparing DNA, we would look at individual bases. If we were comparing manuscripts, we would compare readings. But we are comparing phases of a tale. For this, we compare motifs.

Take, as a very simple example, the name of our hero. In the classical legend, it is "Orpheus" (Latin) or "Ορφεος/Orpheos" (Greek). In *Sir Orfeo* the name is "Orfeo," which is clearly a form of the same thing. In "King Orfeo" there is no name.

Now consider. The Greek legend, of course, came first — that at least is not open to question. Suppose the ballad came second, and it dropped the name "Orpheus." How, then, could the name "Orfeo" have come to be used in the romance?

The answer is, it couldn't. At least as far as the name "Orfeo" is concerned, the romance cannot be descended from the ballad. Either the ballad is descended from the romance or the ballad is descended from the original legend. These are the only possibilities.

We can conduct this same exercise with every motif. One particular instance doesn't prove much, but many instances do.

| Motif / Theme / Topic | As found in the romance *Sir Orfeo* | As found in the ballad "King Orfeo" | Orpheus Legend |
|---|---|---|---|
| Hero's name | Orfeo | Not given | Orpheus |
| Hero's social position | King | King | Minstrel |
| Wife's name | Heurodis | Isabel/Lisa Bell | Euridice |
| Wife's social position | Queen | Queen | Nymph |
| Hero's instrument | Harp | Pipes | Harp |
| Wife carried off to: | Faërie | Faërie | Hades |
| Captor: | King of Faërie | King of Faërie | King of Hades |
| Period wife is missing | Ten years | Seven years | (briefly) |

| | | | |
|---|---|---|---|
| Orpheus enters underworld by: | rock/stone | rock/stone | tunnel/gate |
| Guardian | Porter | Probably a porter, certainly not a dog | Cerberus |
| In other world, music Orpheus plays is: | Not specified | Notes of joy, notes of noy, Gabber Reel | Not specified |
| Orpheus granted wife | Unconditionally | Unconditionally | Must not look back |
| Orpheus returns to world | Successfully | Successfully | Looks back and loses Euridice |
| Description of return trip | None | None | Ends with loss of Euridice |
| Orpheus in his kingdom finds: | Steward faithful | Worthless nephew to be crowned | No kingdom |
| Ending | Orpheus restored | Orpheus restored | Orpheus turns recluse, later murdered |

There are five possible ways the motifs could match or not match: All three stories could be the same (not very helpful); all three could diverge (again, not very helpful), or two could agree against one in any of three ways: the romance could match the legend, the ballad could match the legend, or the romance could match the ballad. So our technique is simply to count how many items belong in each class. For this purpose, we can treat the name "Heurodis" as equivalent to "Euridice"; it's certainly closer than to "Lisa Bell"! That gives us these results:

- *All Three Agree* (irrelevent/not counted)
- *Romance, Ballad agree against Legend:* Hero's social position, Wife's social position, Wife carried off to, Captor, Period wife is missing, Orpheus enters underworld by, Guardian, Orpheus granted wife, Orpheus returns to world, description of return, ending. *[Total of eleven agreements.]*
- *Romance, Legend agree against Ballad:* Hero's name, Wife's name, Hero's instrument, Music Orpheus plays. *[Total of four agreements.]*

- *Legend, Ballad agree against Romance: [No such agreements.]*
- *All Three Disagree:* Orpheus in his kingdom finds. *[One instance]*

This is amazingly clear-cut. We have fifteen tests, and in every one of them, *Sir Orfeo* agrees with one of the other two against the third. There are no agreements at all between the ballad and the legend. If we show relationships as links between items, there is only one possible linkage:

Legend •——• *Sir Orfeo* •——• "King Orfeo"

*Sir Orfeo* is, without question, the middle element—the link—between the legend and "King Orfeo."

But this doesn't tell us the *direction* of the linkages, just what goes where. (The technical term for this is an "unrooted tree."[133]) It can be shown, according to a mathematical formula known as Cayley's Theorem, that there are three actual lines of descent based on a three-node tree. To take that out of the language of math, that means that the above graph allows any of three possible interpretations or genealogies:

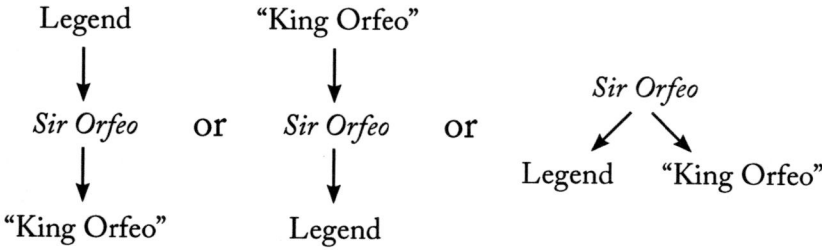

To put the genealogy into words, the possibilities are:

1. The Orpheus legend could be the inspiration of the romance *Sir Orfeo,* which could be the inspiration of the ballad "King Orfeo."

2. "King Orfeo" could be the origin of *Sir Orfeo,* which gave rise to the legend.

3. *Sir Orfeo* could be the ancestor of the other two, which both derived from it independently.

But although these three trees are all possible based on the motif data, *they are not all historically possible.* The Latin legend cannot derive from a Middle English romance; Middle English did not exist when Virgil and Ovid wrote. So any version which makes *Sir Orfeo* or "King Orfeo" the ancestor of the legend can be eliminated on linguistic grounds.

Only one conclusion is possible if we assume the three are related: that the legend gave rise to *Sir Orfeo*, which gave rise to "King Orfeo."

There is, to be sure, one other possibility. Since "King Orfeo" never names its hero, it's possible that it's an independent riff on the wife-stolen-by-fairies theme — a very common folklore theme.[134]

In some ways, "King Orfeo" looks more like a variant on something like "The Queen of Elfand's Nourice" than the Orpheus legend — both have a wife carried off by fairies. Another link between ballad and romance — the grey stone as entrance to Faërie found in 5b of the ballad — is found in several other Celtic tales as well.

The change from harp to pipes is a significant one, since the pipes are not an instrument for singing. Nor are there many similarities in the wording of the romance and the ballad; although *Sir Orfeo* and "King Orfeo" are both in couplets, that style is not rare enough in the romances to mean much.

Some of the other common motifs could be simply coincidence. The Orpheus legend is widespread enough that Stith Thompson made it his motif F81.1; he actually finds a Native American tale which includes the taboo about looking back,[135] and *that* story surely is not related! (The looking-back motif is also found in the tale of Lot's Wife in Genesis 19:26.)

Thus the effects of most of the changes in the legend are to make it more a tale of Faërie and far less a tale grounded in our world, and such changes could happen independently.

Still — in a ballad with 57 lines, we have 11 coincidences with *Sir Orfeo*. That's a substantial list.

Note that "King Orfeo" had an unnamed hero in all the versions, and that he played pipes rather than a stringed instrument, allowing for the possibility that "King Orfeo" might be an independent creation. But the list of motifs shows how close are *Sir Orfeo* and "King Orfeo." The dependence is real: Somehow, the Orpheus legend gave rise to *Sir Orfeo*, and somehow that, or at least its Scottish cousin derived from *Sir Orfeo* or from the same lost original, gave rise to "King Orfeo."

## CHAPTER 6
# *Conclusions and Suggestions for Further Research*

It is usually asserted that ballads are transmitted by oral tradition, while romances are transmitted by written tradition.[136] Both these statements are dubious. The magnum opus by G. Malcolm Laws did much to show the influence of broadside prints on folk songs,[137] and commercial recordings played a major role in spreading folk music abroad.[138] Most of the Robin Hood "ballads" were circulated primarily in print, in the seventeenth and eighteenth century garlands; one, "A True Tale of Robin Hood," was written by Martin Parker and was clearly distributed on paper.[139] The influence of books like the Robin Hood garlands and the *Forget-Me-Not Songster* is far greater than most folk song scholars tend to admit.[140]

The notion that the romances survived via writing is somewhat better founded—their sheer length proves it. *Sir Gawain and the Green Knight* is 2530 lines long.[141] *Ywain and Gawain* clocks in at a hefty 4032 lines.[142] *Guy of Warwick* and *Ipomedon A* clock in at about ten thousand lines. Such works are unlikely to be preserved solely by oral tradition. Other examples of romances unlikely to survive orally can be found in the appendix. In any case, *Sir Gawain* is simply too fine not to have come from the hand of a skilled, unsung *writing* poet.

But not all romances are so long. *Sir Orfeo* is only 604 lines—the equivalent of 151 stanzas. Long, but shorter than some things Child calls ballads. And, what's more, it shows significant indications of oral transmission.[143] We can see this by a comparison of Sisam's text (mostly from the Auchinleck manuscript, supplemented by Harley) and Rumble's (mostly from Ashmole). Some examples:

- Rumble's text begins with the line "Mery tyme is in Aperelle, That mekyll schewes of many wyle"—"In April is a merry time That shows much of men's desires." This conventional opening gives every sign of floating in from somewhere else.
- Rumble's text omits the references to Orfeo's ancestry (Sisam, ll. 29-30)—just the sort of thing scuttled by oral tradition.

- In Sisam (line 52), the queen is "Dame He(u)rodis;" in Rumble (line 44), "Dame Meroudys." It is just possible that Rumble's reading could have arisen by a dittography (the letter "m" written twice), but it is much more likely an error of hearing.
- The story begins at the beginning of May (Sisam, l. 57=Sands, l. 32; Rumble, l. 49), yet the the Sisam and Rumble texts of the next four lines are entirely different, and both versions show signs of borrowings from other poems.
- In line 346, we have an interesting reference to how Orfeo pursued the Faërie folk. Sisam and Burrow/Turville-Petre here read (line 346) "He no spard noiþer stub no ston" (compare Laskaya/Salisbury, line 346, and Sands, line 320, "He no spard noither stub no ston"): "He no spared neither stump nor stone," but Rumble (line 347) has "He sparyd nother stoke ne ston," "He spared neither stock nor stone." The meaning is effectively identical, but the latter reading comes straight out of the minstrel's grab-bag of standard lines—in *Pearl*, for instance, we read "We meten so selden by stok other stone," "we meet so seldom by stock or stone."[144] The displacement of original texts by such cliché readings is a commonplace of oral tradition.
- The number of small dislocations of order are too numerous to count.[145]

Such a long list supplies strong evidence. *Sir Orfeo* may never have been "folk" in the sense of passed orally from person to person, but it clearly was passed from minstrel to minstrel, and the surviving manuscripts are derived from copies *made from different minstrel renditions*. The only difference between this and a folk ballad lies in the fact that the minstrels were professionals.

This suggests that it may be time to rethink our definitions. The boundary between romance and ballad is already rather blurry—Child himself placed three Robin Hood romances among the ballads,[146] and several of his other "ballads," including several from the Percy Folio, have romance-like characteristics. On the other hand, Child clearly acknowledged that some ballads were the work of minstrels.[147]

Carl Lindahl observed that English romances, in particular, took on the ballad characteristic of letting events explain their motivations instead of describing the motivations so as to explain the events.[148] Perhaps, instead of "romances" and "ballads," we should divide into three classes, "written romances," "oral romances," and "ballads." Or even, just possibly, a fourfold division, "written romances," "oral (minstrel) romances," "minstrel ballads" (poems similar to the ballads in form but generally the province of a small set of professionals; these would probably tend to be longer and more formal than our traditional ballads), and the true traditional ballads. The lines between the genres are of course very fluid, but this emphasizes how easily an item can travel from one mode to the other.

It is interesting to consider the contents of manuscripts such as the Auchinleck manuscript containing *Sir Orfeo*, or the Percy Folio, or Richard Calle's manuscript containing *Robin Hood and the Potter*, or even John de Grimestone's manuscript of mostly religious items. It is tempting to simply label them "miscellanies." Yet even miscellanies are assembled for a purpose.

Consider the *Percy Folio*. It contains items that are clearly ballads, and very common ones, such as "Lord Barnard and the Little Musgrave,"[149] "Captaine Carre,"[150] "King John and the Bishoppe,"[151] and "Robin Hood and the Butcher."[152] But the folio also includes undeniable romances, such as "Eger and Grine,"[153] "Merline,"[154] "Sir Lambewell,"[155] "Eglamore,"[156] and "Libius Disconius."[157] And it contains items that, in their current state, might be regarded as either—consider the short form of *The Squire of Low Degree*, *The Turke and Gowin*, *The Marriage of Sir Gawaine*. Clearly the compiler of the folio did not think in our terms.

Other manuscripts are different in detail but also have mixes of types. Richard Calle's miscellany, Cambridge University Library MS. EE.4.35, contains two short romances, "Robyn Hode and the Potter" and "The Kynge and the Barker"; a ballad-like piece, "The Adulterous Falmouth Squire"; a wonder story, "The Miracle of the Lady Who Buried the Host," and a number of other religious and educational items.[158] It looks like a grab bag for a performer who also wanted to be able to teach certain subjects.

The manuscript containing *Sir Gawain and the Carle of Carlisle* "is truly a miscellany, containing lyrics, Christmas carols, prophesies, prognostications, a chronicle, meteorological, astrological, botanical, and agricultural tracts, moral, devotional, and instructional writings, a saint's life, popular bawdy tales, and a prose romance."[159]

Richard Hill's manuscript, which is a personal collection of things he found of interest, has a big chunk of Gower, plus a version of *The Seven Sages of Rome*, many proverbs and instructional poems, some religious materials, and quite a few good carols.[160]

The Auchinleck manuscript which is our main source for *Sir Orfeo* contains many romances (*The King of Tars, Sir Degaré, Floris and Blancheflour,* two tales of *Guy of Warwick, Bevis of Hampton, Arthur and Merlin, Lay le Freine, Sir Otuel, Horne Child,* and others). There are no clear ballads, but there are saints' lives (*Seyte Mergrete, Seynt Keterine*), theological and pseudo-historical works (*The Disputation Between the Body and the Soul, The Assumption of the Blessed Virgin, The Life of Adam and Eve*), saying sources (*The Sayings of St. Bernard*), a history (an anonymous metrical chronicle), and more.[161] This may not be a minstrel's collection, but it is the collection of someone who gives various types of public performance.

That performers should collect a wide variety of materials makes sense. No minstrel could make a living on romances alone. A long romance like *Sir Gawain and the Green Knight* would be an all-day (or multiple-day) performance, and would probably be recited rather than sung. A medium-length item like *Sir Orfeo* would run through a normal dinner. *The Tournament of Tottenham* or *Robin Hood and the Potter* would last about as long as a single course of a meal, and the performer could play the harp or viol for the entire length of the performance. But there would still be need for short pieces — for example, as a course was brought in, or for some sort of a procession, or to fill time, or to cover a number of topics quickly. A minstrel's repertoire would *have to* include ballad-like pieces — as well as other things that aren't either romances or ballads; in the sixteenth century, e.g., a wandering performer might not merely sing and act and recite but also expound "philosophy both morall and naturall."[162]

But then how does the *minstrel* distinguish a ballad from a romance? By how long they last? In that case, our distinction is entirely arbitrary.

The logic wends further. It seems very likely that there were ballads in the High Middle Ages. In a period when people's main entertainments were stories and music, it seems inevitable that they would have had stories *in* music. But the songs of the common folk might well not have been preserved. The surviving ballad-like materials are very likely just as much minstrel work as are the romances.

There is another interesting point here. Although *Sir Orfeo* and "King Orfeo" tell the same story, in many other instances we find a ballad which has only the final scene of the romance. This is the case also with *King Horn* and "Hind Horn,"[163] and with *Floris and Blancheflour* and "Blancheflour and Jellyflorice."[164] It is also, to some extent, the case with *The Gest of Robyn Hode* and "Robin Hood's Death," although in that case the ballad has more details of the event it describes than the romance. It may also have happened with *Guy of Warwick* and the story of *Reinbrun*, who is Guy's son.[165] All this suggests that there might have been truncated versions of romances which were eventually converted to ballads.

An even more interesting instance is *The Squire of Low Degree,* since the *Percy Folio* contains a much-shortened version of the romance. Nor is this the only romance to exist in a shortened version in the Folio; *Eger and Grine* also exists in two states, with the Folio having the shorter version. Perhaps we should look at these instances in a little more detail. Having established that, in the case of the Orfeo texts at least, the ballad is dependent on the romance, what happens if we turn to other romance-and-ballad pairs?

The discussions in this chapter are not intended to be comprehensive; not every romance-and-ballad pair is discussed, and the few I have examined are examined only casually. But they may give us a direction for further work.

## *The Blancheflour Legend*

The romance, in this case, is "Floris and Blancheflour"; the ballad is "Blancheflour and Jellyflorice" [Child 300]. The former exists in four copies, from the thirteenth and fourteenth centuries[166] (or perhaps, in one case, the fifteenth century);[167] this relatively large number of manuscripts may well indicate strong popularity. There is a French original, existing in two states, one more aristocratic and one more popular. The English romance is based on the aristocratic French version, although substantially shortened.[168] It was probably created in the mid-thirteenth century. The manuscripts of the English romance differ substantially; this is another case where it has been suggested that there was a phase of oral transmission.[169]

This is instance where the shorter English version is arguably better than the French version. Although the children always love each, the English text gets rid of the "yuck" factor of two pre-adolescents being educated in "the joy of love" and being seen to "kiss and cuddle one another."[170]

The ballad version is a much more obscure item; it was published by Peter Buchan in 1828, and is from William Motherwell's manuscript. No other copy is known, and no tune has survived. It almost seems like the sort of thing a minstrel would have made up to use as a filler.

Child observed that the ballad used only one incident of the romance, in which Floris saves Blancheflour—and adds that this version does not occur in the English version of the romance![171] Nonetheless the names alone indicate literary dependence; "Blancheflour" is a rare name. It is not obvious why the ballad renamed Floris "Jellyflourice."

Given the French original, it seems safe to assume that the romance precedes the ballad—but there is a fair likelihood that the person responsible for the English ballad knew a French version, extracted the ending, and wrote from there.

## *The Horn Legend*

There are two romances of the "Horn" legend, *King Horn* and *Horn Childe*, with the former being the older and more important. *King Horn* is, in fact, thought to be the oldest surviving Middle English romance. The earliest of the three copies, Cambridge University Library MS. Gg 4.27.2, was written around 1250. The other copies are British Library MS. Harleian 2253 and Bodleian MS. Laud Misc. 108.[172] The story is originally Scandinavian; there is no known French version.

Technically the romance is far from skillful; it is in rhymed lines, but the lines are short—usually three stresses and six syllables, a structure perhaps derived from Old English poetry.[173] These short lines give a very abrupt feeling; it is an uncomfortable form even if you ignore the fact that the poem cannot decide whether to use trochaic or iambic feet. It also uses rather odd place names such as "Suddene" and "Westernesse."

The ballad "Hind Horn" is primarily Scottish, and is fairly well-known there; Child had nine versions[174] and Bronson some two dozen tunes, all related and mostly from Scotland or northeastern North America.[175] Such lack of variation usually implies a fairly close relationship to the original.

The characters in the romance are Horn (a rare and characteristic name) and Rymenhild; the ballad typically features Horn and Jean (so Child's A, C, D, F) or Horn and no name (Child B, E, G, H)

The ballad features only one incident of the romance—what Child calls the "catastrophe"[176] and Tolkien would probably call the "eucatastrophe."

On this evidence, it would appear that either the ballad is worn down from the romance or the romance incorporated the ballad. But could the ballad be from before 1250? Even if ballads existed that long ago, the fact that the versions are all so closely related makes this conclusion difficult. Based on the evidence, *King Horn* preceded, and is the source of, "Hind Horn."

## *The Squire of Low Degree*

The full form of this romance does not survive in manuscript; what we have are printed copies. The only complete edition was printed by William Copeland after 1555; there is also a partial print by Wynken de Worde which may well have been Copeland's source.[177] The language of the *Squire* as it now exists is quite modern, but we know that de Worde often modernized the texts he printed.[178] Copeland was also a modernizer.[179] So we cannot really date the original very closely based on the language.

The full form of the *Squire* is 1131 lines, in couplets; it "is one of the pleasantest and most fluent examples of this verse [form] in English. There is a pause at the end of every line, and the effect is like that of some ballads."[180]

In the *Percy Folio* a version of the *Squire* of only 170 lines[181] — short enough, in other words, to be counted as a ballad. Can this be considered as a ballad relative of the romance? It does contain a small amount of material not in the romance. The likeliest explanation for this, however, is probably simply that it is abridged from a slightly different state of the romance. Unlike most of the other ballad-and-romance pairs, the short form of the *Squire* looks like is is a deliberate recension of the romance, not simply an allusion to the story in the older telling.

So far, we have examined four ballad-and-romance pairs. The conclusions are as follows:

*Sir Orfeo* — the romance inspired the ballad

*Floris and Blancheflour* — the romance inspired the ballad

*King Horn* — the romance inspired the ballad

*The Squire of Low Degree* — the romance is the direct source of the ballad.

That's four instances, and in every case the romance came first.

We must be cautious. This is only four examples, and the only one fully tested was *Sir Orfeo*. But the implication — the hypothesis to be further examined — is that ballads usually derive from romances, not vice versa.

This raises the question: Is there a mechanism for this? That is, is there a means by which romances become ballads? It is not just simple abridgment (apart from *The Squire of Low Degree,* anyway); what survives the transition is more motifs than words. The answer to this will require a more detailed study.

The existence of romance-and-ballad pairs might solve another mystery: the many instances of ballads with foreign equivalents. How many people, in the sixteenth through nineteenth century era when most ballads came into being, had the skills to translate a ballad between languages? And if they did, why didn't the tunes stay the same? Ballads in translation are very improbable things. But we know romances were translated. Could the multilingual ballads in fact be the ballad derivatives, independently created, of romances that were translated? Or even of foreign ballads being made into romances and then translated? It could happen — we know that, in other languages, ballads could be made into romances and vice versa.[182]

One other minor mystery is the role of the *Percy Folio* in all this. Important as this manuscript is, it is curious how often it preserves one half of a romance-and-ballad pair — indeed, in one case, it preserves both!

It contains both a copy of *Sir Eglamore of Artois* and "Sir Lionel." It also has the short version of *The Squire of Low Degree,* found only in it, and the earliest version of "Robin Hood's Death" [Child 120], which parallels the ending of *The Gest of Robyn Hode.* It has a short version of *Eger and Grine.* It has "King Arthur and King Cornwall" [Child 30], which looks like it might be a romance with a lost ballad analogy, and it has "Sir Aldingar," which looks like the ballad half of a pair, with *Octavian* perhaps being the full form. It has been suggested that the folio's *Sir Lambewell* is a reduced version of *Sir Launfal.*[183] It is almost as if the compiler was trying to make up sets of these things — or worked from someone else's set of romance summaries.

Furthermore, why is it that ballads so often parallel the *endings* of romances? It occurs in *The Gest of Robyn Hode*/"Robin Hood's Death," with *King Horn*/"Hind Horn," and with *Floris and Blancheflour*/"Blancheflour and Jellyflorice."

Child weighed these questions, a little, when he looked at some of the romance-and-ballad pairs. But he never reached an overall conclusion[184] — he didn't have the tools available today. Editors since his time have better editions of the romances, and collectors have found many more texts of the ballads. We also have better methods for investigating textual kinship. Now all we need is more work on the data.

One thing seems clear: Many of the romances were the possession of the minstrels—and so were some of the ballads, particularly those in sources such as the *Percy Folio*. What is necessary is a look at the ballads—especially the early ballads which have not been recovered in oral tradition—in that light.

## APPENDIX I
# *List of Middle English Romances*

The catalog below is compiled from diverse sources,[185] some of which include nothing more than the name of the romances they cite; it is intended to be inclusive, and so lists some items rarely regarded as romances—although it omits a few pieces, such as the English version of the *Song of Roland,* which are clearly *chansons* and not romances. Prose romances such as *Blanchardyn and Eglantine* and the work of Malory are omitted. The list cites possible ballad analogues where known; romances with analogues are listed first. Most romances have not been examined in detail for analogues. In the list below, the common name of the romance is shown first, then its format—the number of lines and the structure. Information about the sources follows, then a list of editions used to check the characteristics of the romance (if it has been checked).[186] Then comes the ballad analogue if any. The second item, for instance, is

2. **Floris and Blancheflour**
   DIMEV #3686
   Format: 1083/1225 lines, couplets
   Copies of English version: 4 MSS., all incomplete
   Original Source: 2 Old French versions
   Modern Editions: Donald B. Sands, editor, *Middle English Verse Romances*, p. 279; Erik Kooper, *Sentimental and Humorous Romances,* TEAMS, available online
   Notes: Independent of major romance cycles. See discussion above.
   Ballad Analogue: Blancheflour and Jellyflorice [Child 300]

Translated, this means that the romance *Floris and Blancheflour* is #3686 in the Digital Index of Middle English Verse (DIMEV) is 1083 lines long in the first edition checked, (Sands)[187] and 1225 in the second (Kooper, in the TEAMS archive online[188]). The poetic form used is couplets. There are four manuscript copies, none of which is complete. There are two Old French versions, one of which is in this case the likely original on which the translation is based. Information is derived from the editions by Sands and Kooper. The notes give some background; these discussions are not intended to be comprehensive. There is a ballad analogue, Child #300, "Blancheflour and Jellyflorice."

Items marked with an asterisk are included in the Auchinleck manuscript which also contains the earliest copy of *Sir Orfeo*. † indicates an item in the *Percy Folio*.

1. †**Eger and Grime**
   (no DIMEV number)
   Format: 2860 lines, couplets
   Copies of English version: 1 printed copy, from 1711
   Modern Editions: Hales and Furnival, *Eger and Grime: An Early English Romance*, p. 18
   Notes: The introduction to the Hales and Furnival text provides hints that this was perhaps sung to the tune "Gray Steel." Chivalric love tale, unconnected with the major romance cycles.
   Ballad Analogue: Short form of "Eger" [1472 lines] found in the †Percy Folio {DIMEV #4191}

2. *****Floris and Blancheflour**
   DIMEV #3686
   Format: 1083/1225 lines, couplets; incomplete
   Copies of English version: 4 MSS.
   Original Source: 2 Old French versions
   Modern Editions: Donald B. Sands, editor, *Middle English Verse Romances*, p. 279; Erik Kooper, *Sentimental and Humorous Romances*, TEAMS, available online
   Notes: Independent of major romance cycles.
   Ballad Analogue: Blancheflour and Jellyflorice [Child 300]

3. **The Gest of Robyn Hode**
   DIMEV #3129
   Format: 1824? lines, couplets
   Copies of English version: 3 complete and 4 fragmentary prints
   Modern Editions: Child, vol. III, p. 39, item #121; p. 115; R. B. Dobson and J. Taylor, *Rymes of Robyn Hood: An Introduction to the English Outlaw*, p. 71; Stephen Knight and Thomas Ohlgren, editors, *Robin Hood and Other Outlaw Tales*, p. 80; Waltz, *The Gest of Robyn Hode*
   Ballad Analogue (partial): Robin Hood's Death [Child 120]

4. *****(Stanzaic) Guy of Warwick A**
   DIMEV #4907, #6734
   Format: 3587 lines, 12-line tail rhyme
   Copies of English version: 3 MSS.
   Original Source: from the Anglo-Norman *Gui de Warewic*
   Modern Editions: Alison Wiggins, *Stanzaic Guy of Warwick*, TEAMS, available online
   Notes: Other Guy romances are *Guy of Warwick B* and *Reinbrun*
   Ballad Analogue: Two items from the †Percy Folio, "Guy & Phyllis" (a short version of the whole tale) and "Guy & Colbrande" (a short version of Guy's fight with a giant)

5. **Guy of Warwick B**
   DIMEV #4908
   Format: 11976 lines, couplets
   Copies of English version: 1 MS, Cambridge University Library Ff.2.38
   Notes: Other Guy romances are *Guy of Warwick A* and *Reinbrun*. Probably fifteenth century, making it more recent than *Guy* A.
   Ballad Analogue: see the notes under Guy of Warwick A

6. **King Edward and the Shepherd/The King and the Barker/etc.**
   DIMEV #6691, etc.
   Format: varies; usually couplets
   Notes: General plot exists in many forms
   Ballad Analogue: King Edward the Fourth and a Tanner of Tamworth [Child 273]

7. **King Horn**
   DIMEV #312
   Format: 1542/1546/1544 lines, couplets, very short lines
   Copies of English version: 3 MSS.
   Modern Editions: Sands, p. 15; Joseph Ritson, *Ancient English Metrical Romances*, revised by Edmund Goldsmid, vol. 2, p. 99; Herzman, Drake, and Salisbury, *Four Romances of England*, TEAMS, available online
   Notes: Probably the earliest Middle English romance. Unrelated to other romance cycles. Compare the romance *Horne Childe*.
   Ballad Analogue: Hind Horn [Child 17]

8. ***Horn Childe [and Maid(en) Rimnild]**
   DIMEV #3622
   Format: 1138 surviving lines, modified 12-line tail rhyme, *aabaabcccbccb*. Incomplete
   Copies of English version: 1 MS., *Auchinleck MS/Advocates 19.2.1
   Modern Editions: Ritson/Goldsmid, vol. 2, p. 216
   Notes: Compare the romance *King Horn*. Unrelated to other romance cycles.
   Ballad Analogue: Hind Horn [Child 17]

9. ***Lay Le Freine**
   DIMEV #6173
   Format: 408 lines in most editions, but 80 of these are reconstructions based on the French version to fill a lacuna in the surviving manuscript; couplets
   Copies of English version: 1 MS., *Auchinleck MS/Advocates 19.2.1
   Original Source: based on Marie of France's *Lay Le Friene*
   Modern Editions: Sands, p. 233; Rumble, p. 81; Anne Laskaya and Eve Salisbury, *The Middle English Breton Lays*, TEAMS, available online
   Notes: Preface is the same as the preface found in many versions of *Sir Orfeo*. A tale of an extramarital romance, unrelated to the major romance cycles.
   Ballad Analogue: Fair Annie [Child 62][189]

10. **†Libeaus Desconus (The Fair Unknown)**
    DIMEV #2824
    Format: 2130/2252 lines, 12-line tail rhyme with very short lines
    Copies of English version: 6 MSS.

Original Source: based on the French *Li Biaus Desconeüs* of Renaud de Beaujeu
Modern Editions: Ritson/Goldsmid, vol. 2, p. 35; George Shuffleton, *Codex Ashmole 61: A Compilation of Popular Middle English Verse*, TEAMS, available online
Notes: sometimes attributed to Thomas Chestre, author of *Sir Launfal*. Arthurian romance, of an illegitimate son of Sir Gawain, who comes to Arthur's court to become a knight.
Ballad Analogue: The Laidley Worm of Spindleston Heugh[190]

11. **Octavian 1 (the "Northern Version")**
    DIMEV #3132
    Format: 1791/1848 lines, 12-line tail rhyme
    Copies of English version: 2 MSS+a damaged print by Wynken de Worde
    Original Source: Old French original
    Modern Editions: Mills, *Six Middle English Romances*, p. 75; Harriet Hudson, *Four Middle English Romances*, TEAMS, available online
    Notes: Compare the Southern Version of *Octavian*. Not about the man who became Augustus Caesar; the story, involving a queen accused of adultery, has some slight links to the life of Diocletian.
    Ballad Analogue: Should be compared with "Sir Aldingar" [Child 59]; there is an accusation of adultery and a mother-in-law who induces a servant to sleep naked in the lady's bed. Probably not the same item, but with links to a possible common source.

12. **Octavian 2 (the "Southern Version")**
    DIMEV #2930
    Format: 1962? lines; 6-line stanzas rhyming *aaabab*
    Copies of English version: 1 MS., Bodleian, MS Cotton Caligula A.ii
    Notes: Sometimes attributed to Thomas Chestre, author of *Sir Launfal*. The tale, and the ballad equivalents, are the same as the Northern Version of *Octavian*; it is a shorter translation of the same French original.

13. **†Sir Eglamore of Artois**
    DIMEV #2867
    Format: 1291/1320 lines; 12-line tail rhyme
    Copies of English version: 6 MSS. plus 5 prints
    Modern Editions: John W. Hales & Frederick J. Furnivall, *Bishop Percy's Folio Manuscript: Ballads and Romances*, v. 3, p. 9; Harriet Hudson, *Four Middle English Romances*, TEAMS, available online
    Notes: A tale of a knight of low standing loving a woman of higher degree, not related to the major romance cycles. To this compare the lost "The Forester and the Wild Boar" (Wilson, *Lost Literature*, p. 129).
    Ballad Analogue: Sir Lionel [Child 18]. Compare also the later romance of *Sir Torrent of Portyngale*, which may have been influenced by *Sir Eglamore* and which, unlike most romances, was taken down from oral tradition.

14. **Sir Gawain and the Carle of Carlisle**
    DIMEV #3110 (see also "Carle off Calisle")
    Format: 660 lines, 12-line tail rhyme
    Copies of English version: 1 MS., NL Wales Porkington 10

Modern Editions: Thomas Hahn, editor, *Sir Gawain: Eleven Romances and Tales*, p. 81; also TEAMS, available online; Sands, p. 348
Notes: Clearly of northern origin
Ballad Analogue: possibly "Carle off Carlisle," in the †Percy Folio (Hahn, p. 373). which is also listed as a romance below

15. **Sir Launfal** {by Thomas Chestre}
    DIMEV #930
    Format: 1044 lines, 12-line tail rhyme
    Copies of English version: 1 MS., BL Cotton Caligula A.ii
    Original Source: derived from *Sir Landevale* with additions from Old French *Graelant*
    Modern Editions: Rumble, p. 3; Sands, p. 201; Ritson/Goldsmid, vol. 2, p. 1; Anne Laskaya and Eve Salisbury, *The Middle English Breton Lays*, TEAMS, available online
    Notes: Arthurian romance, with a chivalrous knight repeatedly slighted and forced to prove his prowess
    Ballad Analogue: "Sir Lambewell," in the †Percy Folio — almost certainly a derivative of this piece, but only 632 lines, in couplets

16. ***Sir Orfeo**
    DIMEV #6172
    Format: 580/604 lines, couplets
    Copies of English version: 3 MSS.
    Modern Editions: Burrow/Turville-Petre, p. 114; Rumble ["Kyng Orfew"], p. 207; Sands, p. 185; Sisam, p. 14; Anne Laskaya and Eve Salisbury, *The Middle English Breton Lays*, TEAMS, available online; George Shuffleton, *Codex Ashmole 61: A Compilation of Popular Middle English Verse*, TEAMS, available online; modernization by Tolkien; prose version in Loomis/Loomis[191]
    Ballad Analogue: King Orfeo [Child 19]

17. **(†)The Squire of Low Degree**
    DIMEV #2762
    Format: 1132 lines, couplets
    Copies of English version: 1 print by Copeland, 1555-1560, 1 fragment of early XVI
    Modern Editions: Sands, p. 249; Erik Kooper, *Sentimental and Humorous Romances*, TEAMS, available online
    Ballad Analogue: Short form of the "Squire" [170 lines] found in the †Percy Folio

18. **The Tale of Florent** (by John Gower; part of the *Confessio Amantis*)
    DIMEV #4226 (for the "A" text), #4227 ("B"), #4228 ("C"), #4229 (fragments)
    Format: 475 lines, couplets
    Copies of English version: 68 total witnesses to the *Confessio*, not all containing this part of the poem
    Modern Editions: Russell A. Peck with Andrew Galloway; John Gower, *Confessio Amantis, Volume I*, second edition, TEAMS, available online
    Notes: very possibly one of Chaucer's sources for the *Wife of Bath's Tale*
    Ballad Analogue: The Marriage of Sir Gawain [Child 31] (Child I, p. 288; Hahn, p. 359). Note: "The Marriage of Sir Gawain" is in the †Percy Folio. Half of it is missing, but the length argues that it should perhaps be listed as a romance rather than a ballad.

19. **The Wedding of Sir Gawain and Dame Ragnell**
    DIMEV #3130
    Format: 855 lines extant, 6-line tail rhyme; probably 70 lines missing after line 628; some other lines lost due to scribal error; it is very poorly written
    Copies of English version: 1 fragmentary MS., Bodleian 11951/Rawlinson C.86
    Modern Editions: Hahn, p. 47; Sands, p. 323
    Notes: A Loathly Woman tale, of the same materials as the *Wife of Bath's Tale* and the *Tale of Florent*
    Ballad Analogue: The Marriage of Sir Gawain [Child 31]; see description under *The Tale of Florent*

20. **The Wife of Bath's Tale** (by Geoffrey Chaucer)
    DIMEV #2618
    Format: 408 lines, couplets
    Modern Editions: Larry D. Benson, general editor, *The Riverside Chaucer*, third edition, p. 116
    Notes: A "Loathly Woman" tale with close relatives in the *Tale of Florent* and the *Wedding of Sir Gawain and Dame Ragnell*
    Ballad Analogue: The Marriage of Sir Gawain [Child 31]; see description under *The Tale of Florent*

21. ***Amis and Amiloun***[192]
    DIMEV #1350
    Format: 2508 lines, 12-line modified tail rhyme, *aabaabccdeed*
    Copies of English version: 4 MSS
    Modern Editions: Edward E. Foster, *Amis and Amiloun, Robert of Cisyle, and Sir Amadace*, TEAMS, available online
    Notes: A friendship romance, with disguise elements, unrelated to the major romance cycles

22. **Amoryus and Cleopes** (by John Metham, 1449)
    DIMEV #5231
    Format: 2222 lines, seven-line stanzas, *ababbcc*
    Copies of English version: 1 MS, Princeton MS Garrett 141
    Original Source: based on Ovid's tale of Pyramus and Thisbe, perhaps with an intermediate stage which improved the ending; there are elements from Chaucer, who inspired the stanza form
    Modern Editions: Stephen F. Page, editor, *John Metham, Amoryus and Cleopes*, TEAMS, available online
    Notes: A love romance unrelated to the major romance cycles

23. **Apollonius of Tyre**
    DIMEV #4829
    Format: 140 lines remaining of an original estimated at about 3000; quatrains rhymed *abab*
    Copies of English version: 1 MS, Bodleian Library MS Douce 216
    Notes: Shakespeare's *Pericles* derives from this tale, which is unrelated to the major romance cycles.

24. **Athelston**
    DIMEV #3226
    Format: 812 lines, 12-line tail rhyme
    Copies of English version: 1 MS., Gonville and Caius 175
    Modern Editions: Sands, p. 130; Herzman, Drake, and Salisbury, *Four Romances of England*, TEAMS, available online
    Notes: About an English lord, but not King Athelstan; unrelated to the major romance cycles, it is about an errant monarch corrected by the Church and others.

25. *†**Arthour and Merlin**
    DIMEV #2807 and 1886
    Format: 9938 lines, couplets
    Copies of English version: 5 MSS, but none except *Auchinleck contains more than 2400 lines; 2 early prints
    Original Source: Based on the French vulgate Arthur cycle
    Modern Editions: John W. Hales & Frederick J. Furnivall, *Bishop Percy's Folio Manuscript*, 3 volumes, N. Trübner & Co., 1867 and after, vol. 1, p. 401; available on Google Books
    Notes: Often regarded as two romances on an Arthurian theme. The fragmentary state of the MSS makes it hard to be sure.

26. **The Avowying of Arthur**
    DIMEV #1885
    Format: 1148 lines, modified 16-line tail rhyme with the form *aaabcccbdddbeeeb* with irregular line lengths
    Copies of English version: 1 MS, Princeton, Robert H. Taylor MS. Ireland Blackburn
    Modern Editions: Hahn, p. 113

27. **The Awntyrs off Arthur/The Anturs of Arther**
    DIMEV #2628
    Format: 715 lines, 13-line stanzas, first nine lines of each stanza alliterative, rhymed *ababababcdddc*
    Copies of English version: 4 MSS.
    Modern Editions: Hahn, p. 171; Maldwyn Mills, *Ywain and Gawain*, p. 161

28. ***Bevis of Hampton**
    DIMEV #3250, 5362
    Format: 4620 lines, mixed format; 474 lines in 6-line tail rhyme, 4146 in couplets
    Copies of English version: 6 MSS, plus 5 early prints, so distinct that some editors regard it as two or more romances.
    Original Source: from the Anglo-Norman *Boeuve de Haumton*
    Modern Editions: Herzman, Drake, and Salisbury, *Four Romances of England*, TEAMS, available online

29. **Le Bone Florence of Rome**
    DIMEV #575
    Format: 2189 lines, 12-line tail rhyme
    Copies of English version: 1 MS., Cambridge University Library MS. Ff.2.38
    Modern Editions: Joseph Ritson, *Ancient English Metrical Romances, Volume III*, p. 1, available on Google Books

Notes: Florence is a girl of Rome sought by the Emperor of Constantinople. Unrelated to the major romance cycles.

30. **Brut (British "histories")**
Notes: There are several of these, the most important probably by Laȝamon—but although metrical, and largely devoted to the Arthurian legend, they were probably regarded at least partly as history by the hearers. Also, they generally precede our period.

31. **Capystranus**
Format: unknown length, 12-line tail rhyme
Copies of English version: 3 early prints, all by Wynken de Worde, all incomplete
Original Source: probably based on a legend of St. John of Capistrano and the 1456 siege of Belgrade following the fall of Constantinople
Notes: if we had a complete version, we might find that it is not a romance

32. **†The Carle of Carlisle**
DIMEV #3110
Format: 500 lines, couplets
Copies of English version: 1 MS., the †Percy Folio
Modern Editions: Hahn, p. 373
Notes: Possibly should be classed with the ballads; compare *Sir Gawain and the Carle of Carlisle* above

33. **Chevelere Assigne** (The Swan Knight)
DIMEV #417
Format: 370 lines, alliterative
Copies of English version: 1 MS, BL Cotton Caligula A.ii
Modern Editions: Henry H. Gibbs, *The Romance of the Cheuelere Assigne, p. 1*
Notes: A tale of twins, a queen accused of adultery, and the boy who redeems her. Not related to other Romance cycles.

34. **The Destruction of Troy (Geste Historiale)**
DIMEV #3443
Format: 14044 lines, alliterative
Copies of English version: [1 MS, Glasgow University Library MS. Hunterian V.2.8 (388)
Original Source: based on Guido de Colonna's 1287 *Historia Troiana*
Notes: possibly composed by John Clerk of Whalley, Lancashire

35. **The Erle of Tolous**
DIMEV #2813
Format: 1224 lines, modified 12-line tail rhyme
Copies of English version: 4 MSS.
Modern Editions: Rumble, p. 135; Anne Laskaya and Eve Salisbury, *The Middle English Breton Lays*, TEAMS, available online; George Shuffleton, *Codex Ashmole 61*, TEAMS, available online
Notes: Not related to other major romance cycles. The wife of Diocletian Emperor of Germany is accused of adultery but is rescued by the Earl of Tolouse, who later marries her.

36. **Emaré**
    DIMEV #2920
    Format: 1035 lines, 12-line tail rhyme
    Copies of English version: 1 MS., BL Cotton Caligula A.ii
    Modern Editions: Maldwyn Mills, *Six Middle English Romances,* p. 46; Rumble, p. 97; Ritson/Goldsmid, vol. 2, p. 183; Anne Laskaya and Eve Salisbury, *The Middle English Breton Lays,* TEAMS, available online
    Notes: Incest tale, unrelated to the major romance cycles. Emaré's father lusts after her, then exiles her.

37. **The Franklin's Tale** (by Geoffrey Chaucer)
    DIMEV #2476
    Format: 895 lines, couplets
    Modern Editions: Chaucer/Benson, p. 178; Rumble, p. 229

38. **Gamelyn**
    DIMEV #3090
    Format: 902/899 lines, couplets
    Copies of English version: 27 MSS., all of Chaucer, where it is linked with the Cook's Tale
    Modern Editions: Sands, p. 154; Knight/Ohlgren, TEAMS, p. 194, available online
    Notes: An outlaw tale, unrelated to the major romance cycles, of a younger son who wins pardon mostly by brute force

39. **Generides A**
    DIMEV #1111
    Format: 10086 lines, couplets
    Copies of English version: 1 MS., Pierpont Morgan M876
    Notes: A Joseph-in-Egypt type story, of an unknown prince who rebuffs a queen but regains his honor, unrelated to the major romance cycles.

40. **Generides B**
    DIMEV #2557
    Format: 6995 lines, 7-line stanzas, rhymed *ababacc*
    Copies of English version: 2 MSS. plus 3 prints, all defective
    Modern Editions: Frederick J. Furnival, *A Royal Historie of the Excellent Knight Generides,* Henry Huck Gibbs, 1865, p. 1, available on Google Books
    Notes: Same story as Generides A, but an independent telling

41. **†The Greene Knight**
    DIMEV #3088
    Format: 515 lines, 12-line tail rhyme
    Copies of English version: 1 MS., the †Percy folio
    Modern Editions: Hahn, p. 309
    Notes: Same story as *Sir Gawain and the Green Knight,* but clearly not derived directly from that romance.

42. **Havelok the Dane**
    DIMEV #1795
    Format: 3001 lines, couplets

53

Copies of English version: 1 MS, Bodleian, Laud Misc. 108, plus a few fragments
Original Source: n Old French as *Lai d'havelock*
Modern Editions: Sands, p. 55; Skeat, *The Lay of Havelock the Dane,* available on Google Books and Project Gutenberg; Herzman, Drake, and Salisbury, *Four Romances of England,* TEAMS, available online
Notes: A Germanic romance of a displaced prince (Havelok) and the princess Goldborou, unrelated to the major romance cycles

43. **Ipomedon A**
    DIMEV #4183
    Format: 8890 lines, 12-line tail rhyme
    Copies of English version: 1 MS, Manchester MS. Chetham 8009
    Original Source: based on the French *Ipomedon* by Hue de Rotelande
    Recent Editions: Eugen Kölbing, *Ipomedon in drei englischen bearbeitungen,* Verlag von Wilhelm Koebner, 1889, p. 1, available on Google Books

44. **Ipomedon B**
    DIMEV #3462
    Format: 2346 lines, couplets
    Copies of English version: 1 MS, British Library, MS. Harley 2252, plus a print by Wynken de Worde
    Original Source: based on the French *Ipomedon* by Hue de Rotelande
    Modern Editions: Eugen Kölbing, *Ipomedon in drei englischen bearbeitungen,* Verlag von Wilhelm Koebner, 1889, p. 257, available on Google Books

45. **The Jeaste of Sir Gawain**
    DIMEV #306
    Format: 541 extant lines, 6-line tail rhyme
    Copies of English version: incomplete manuscript copy, Bodleian Douce 261, of a print of XVI; also fragments of perhaps as many as 3 prints of XVI
    Modern Editions: Hahn, p. 393

46. **Joseph of Arimathea**
    DIMEV #4864
    Format: 709 lines now extant, alliterative
    Copies of English version: 1 MS, Bodleian Library MS. Eng. Poet. a.1, the Vernon MS; beginning lost
    Modern Editions: Walter W. Skeat, *Joseph of Arimathie, otherwise called The Romance of the Seint Graal, or Holy Grain,* Early English Text Society, 1871, p. 1, available on Google Books
    Notes: A story of how the Joseph brought the Grail to Britain, but not really connected to the Arthurian romance cycle.

47. ***The King of Tars**
    DIMEV #1789
    Format: 1138/1228 lines, 12-line tail rhyme
    Copies of English version: 3 MSS.
    Modern Editions: Ritson/Goldsmid, vol. 2, p. 147

Notes: A story of the beautiful daughter of the King converting the Sultan of Damascus, unrelated to the major romance cycles.

48. **The Knight's Tale** (by Geoffrey Chaucer)
    DIMEV #6530
    Format: 2267 lines, couplets
    Modern Editions: Chaucer/Benson, p. 37

49. **The Knightly Tale of Gologras and Gawain (Golagrus and Gawain)**
    DIMEV #2629
    Format: 1360 lines, 13-line stanzas, first nine lines of each stanza alliterative, rhymed *ababababcdddc*
    Copies of English version: from the Chepman and Millar press, 1508; sole copy preserved in NL Scotland Advocates H.30.a
    Original Source: based on the "first continuation" of Chrétien's *Percival*
    Modern Editions: Hahn, p. 227
    Notes: Scottish dialect, strong enough to make an English origin unlikely.

50. ***King Alisaunder**
    DIMEV #1131
    Format: *c.* 6700 lines, couplets, much damaged
    Copies of English version: 3 MSS plus possible fragments and 1 fragmentary print

51. **Lancelot of the Laik**
    DIMEV #5469
    Format: 3487 lines as now extant; couplets; defective at end and possibly at the beginning.
    Copies of English version: 1 MS., Cambridge University Library MS. Kk.1.5
    Original Source: French original, based on the first part of the vulgate *Lancelot*.
    Modern Editions: Alan Lupack, *Lancelot of the Laik and Sir Tristrem*, TEAMS, available online; W. W. Skeat, *Lancelot of the Laik*, available from Project Gutenberg
    Notes: Scottish; probably composed late in the fifteenth century.

52. **The Merchant's Tale** (by Geoffrey Chaucer)
    DIMEV #6535
    Format: 1273 lines, couplets
    Modern Editions: Chaucer/Benson, p. 154

53. **The Alliterative Morte Arthure**
    DIMEV #3745
    Format: 4346 lines, irregular alliterative lines
    Copies of English version: 1 MS., Lincoln Cathedral Library MS. 91
    Modern Editions: Larry D. Benson, editor, revised by Edward E. Foster, *King Arthur's Death: The Middle English Stanzaic Morte Arthur and Alliterative Morte Arthure*, TEAMS, p. 131, also available online
    Notes: The sole source is the Thornton MS., which is particularly prone to dittographic errors, producing an erratic text. The underlying text is, however, considered one of the best of the alliterative poems of the Middle Ages. It may have chronicle elements. The first half was a major source for Malory.

54. **The Stanzaic Morte Arthure**
    DIMEV #3252
    Format: 3969 lines, 8-line stanzas rhymed *abababab*
    Copies of English version: 1 MS., British Library MS. Harley 2252
    Original Source: much compressed from the French *La Mort Artu*
    Modern Editions: Benson/Foster, *King Arthur's Death: The Middle English Stanzaic Morte Arthur and Alliterative Morte Arthure*, TEAMS, p. 11, also available online
    Notes: One of Malory's leading sources for the ending of his work, which he quotes not infrequently.

55. **Partenope of Blois**
    DIMEV #6533, #6615
    Format: about 12,275 lines, couplets
    Copies of English version: 6 MSS, all incomplete, possibly representing two versions
    Original Source: French, *Parténopeus de Blois*
    Notes: Also called "Parthenope," "Partonope." A variant on the Eros and Psyche legend.

56. **A Pistil of (Sweet) Susan**
    DIMEV #5607
    Format: 364 lines, lliterative with bob-and-wheel, similar to *Sir Gawain and the Green Knight* but with *ababababcdddc* rhymes
    Copies of English version: 5 MSS.
    Original Source: poetic adaption of the Story of Susanna in the Greek additions to Daniel;[193] the story, of a virtuous wife falsely accused, is unrelated to the major romance cycles
    Modern Editions: Thorlac Turville-Petrie, *Alliterative Poetry of the Later Middle Ages: An Anthology*, p. 123; Russell A. Peck, *Heroic Women from the Old Testament in Middle English Verse*, TEAMS, available online

57. **[The Tale of] Rauf Coilyear/Coilȝear** (Ralph the Collier)
    DIMEV #2596
    Format: 972 lines, 13-line stanzas, first nine lines of each stanza alliterative, rhymed *ababababcdddc*
    Copies of English version: 1 print, published by Robert Lekpreuik, 1572
    Modern Editions: Alan Lupack, *Three Middle English Charlemagne Romances*, TEAMS, available online
    Notes: Scottish in language and probably in origin.

58. ***Reinbroun**
    DIMEV #2907
    Format: 1522 lines, 12-line tail rhyme; ending missing
    Copies of English version: 1 MS, *Auchinleck MS/Advocates 19.2.1
    Modern Editions: Julius Zupitza, *The Romance of Guy of Warwick, Part I*, Early English Text Society, 1875, p. 631
    Notes: sequel to one of the Guy of Warwick romances.

59. **Richard Coer de Lion**
    DIMEV #3231

Format: 9000+ lines, couplets
Copies of English version: 8 MSS, all incomplete; 2 early prints.

60. **Robert of Sicily (Cisyle)**
    DIMEV #4415
    Format: 444 lines, couplets
    Copies of English version: 10 MSS.
    Modern Editions: Edward E. Foster, *Amis and Amiloun, Robert of Cisyle, and Sir Amadace*, TEAMS, available online
    Notes: A romance of humility: King Robert is brought low after excessive boasting. Unrelated to the major romance cycles.

61. **Robin Hood and the Monk**
    DIMEV #2586
    Format: 180 lines, couplets
    Copies of English version: 1 MS, Cambridge University Library MS FF.5.48
    Modern Editions: Child, volume III, p. 94, item #119; Dobson/Taylor, p. 113; Knight/Ohlgren, p. 31
    Notes: Usually listed as a ballad rather than a romance, but the metrical form is too loose for singing. A bloody outlaw tale.

62. **Robin Hood and the Potter**
    DIMEV #2585
    Format: 166 lines, couplets
    Copies of English version: 1 MS., Cambridge University Library MS. Ee.4.35 (Richard Calle's MS)
    Modern Editions: Child, volume III, p. 109; item #121; Dobson/Taylor, p. 123; Knight/Ohlgren, p. 57
    Notes: Usually listed as a ballad rather than a romance, but the metrical form is too loose for singing. A humorous outlaw tale.

63. **Roland and Otuel**
    DIMEV #3254
    Format: 1596 lines, 12-line tail rhyme
    Copies of English version: MS., British Library, Additional MS 31042
    Modern Editions: Sidney J. Herrtage, *The English Charlemagne Romances, Part II: "The Sege of Melayne" and "The Romance of Duke Rowland and Sir Otuell of Spayne,"* Early English Text Society, 1880, p. 53; available on Google Books.
    Notes: Charlemagne romance. Cf. "Sir Otuel/Otuel a Knight," a second English translation of the same original.

64. ***Roland and Vernagu**
    DIMEV #1353
    Format: 880 lines now extant, 12-line tail rhyme; beginning lost
    Copies of English version: 1 MS., *Auchinleck MS/Advocates 19.2.1
    Modern Editions: Alexander Nicholson, *Ancient Metrical Romances from the Auchinleck Manuscript: The Romances of Rouland and Vernagu, and Otuel*, available from openlibrary.org, p. 1
    Notes: Charlemagne romance, one of many involving Roland.

65. **The Sege of Melayne (The Siege of Milan)**
    DIMEV #408
    Format: 1599 lines, 12-line tail rhyme; ending lost
    Copies of English version: 1 MS., BL MS. Additional 31042
    Modern Editions: Mills, *Six Middle English Romances*, p. 1; Sidney J. Herrtage, *The English Charlemagne Romances, Part II: "The Sege of Melayne" and "The Romance of Duke Rowland and Sir Otuell of Spayne,"* Early English Text Society, 1880, p. 1; available on Google Books; Alan Lupack, *Three Middle English Charlemagne Romances*, TEAMS, available online.

66. *****The Seven Sages of Rome**
    DIMEV #3187, 4984, 4986, 4987
    Format: about 4328 lines, couplets
    Copies of English version: 9 MSS.
    Original Source: Old French source, from Latin; earliest form of the tale probably from Persia or India
    Modern Editions: Killis Campbell, *The Seven Sages of Rome*, 1907, p. 1, available on Google Books
    Notes: As the DIMEV numbers show, the manuscripts, mostly incomplete, represent several possibly-independent versions of different lengths. This story in its various forms seems to have had very strong popular roots, since both Richard Hill and the Pastons had copies.[194]

67. **Sir Amadace**
    DIMEV #5552
    Format: 840/860 lines, 12-line tail rhyme; beginning lost
    Copies of English version: 2 MSS.
    Modern Editions: Mills, *Six Middle English Romances*, p. 19; Edward E. Foster, *Amis and Amiloun, Robert of Cisyle, and Sir Amadace*, TEAMS, available online
    Notes: A knight loses his fortune but regains it by his courtesy; unrelated to the major romance cycles.

68. **Sir Cleges**
    DIMEV #3093
    Format: 576 lines, 12-line tail rhyme
    Copies of English version: 2 MSS.
    Modern Editions: Anne Laskaya and Eve Salisbury, *The Middle English Breton Lays*, TEAMS, available online; George Shuffleton, *Codex Ashmole 61: A Compilation of Popular Middle English Verse*, TEAMS, available online
    Notes: Not all regard this as a Breton Lai. Set in the time of Uther rather than Arthur. A tale of a poor knight restored.

69. *†**Sir Degaré/Sir Degree (Degore, Digory)**
    DIMEV #3116
    Format: 997/900 lines, couplets
    Copies of English version: 6 MSS.+ 3 early print editions
    Modern Editions: Rumble, p. 45; Hales & Furnival, v. 3, p. 195; Anne Laskaya and Eve Salisbury, *The Middle English Breton Lays*, TEAMS, available online

Notes: Degare, the son of a princess raped by a fairy knight, restores his honor. Unrelated to the major romance cycles.

70. **Sir Degrevant**
DIMEV #3197
Format: 1920 lines, modified 16-line tail rhyme with the form *aaabcccbdddbeeeb;* short lines
Copies of English version: 2 MSS.
Modern Editions: Erik Kooper, *Sentimental and Humorous Romances,* TEAMS, available online
Notes: Of a crusader who restores his fortune after much is stolen during his absence by a neighbor with whom he feuds. Love and battle scenes intermix. Much alliteration. Although Arthur is mentioned, it is not really Arthurian.

71. **Sir Firumbras**
DIMEV #972
Format: 5852 lines, couplets, but the meter changes after line 3410; beginning and end lost
Copies of English version: 1 MS., Bodleian Ashmole 33
Original Source: French original
Modern Editions: Sidney J. Herrtage, *The English Charlemagne Romances, Part I: Sir Ferumbras,* Early English Text Society, 1879, p. 1; available on Google Books

72. **Sir Gawain and the Green Knight**
DIMEV #4920
Format: 2530 lines; alliterative with rhymed "bob and wheel"
Copies of English version: 1 MS., BL Cotton Nero A.x
Modern Editions: J. R. R. Tolkien and E. V. Gordon, *Sir Gawain and the Green Knight,* 2nd edition edited by Norman Davis, p. 1

73. **Sir Gowther**
DIMEV #1595
Format: 750/696/756 lines, 12-line tail rhyme
Copies of English version: 2 MSS.
Modern Editions: Mills, *Six Middle English Romances,* p. 148; Rumble, p. 179; Anne Laskaya and Eve Salisbury, *The Middle English Breton Lays,* TEAMS, available online
Notes: Gowther is the son of the Devil, born when his mother prays for a child at any cost; violent at first, he overcomes his ancestry. Not related to the major romance cycles.

74. **Sir Isumbras**
DIMEV #1934
Format: 798/771/822 lines, 6-line tail rhyme
Copies of English version: at least 4 MSS., possibly as many as 10 counting fragments; 5 printed editions
Original Source: modified from the tale of St. Eustace
Modern Editions: Mills, *Six Middle English Romances,* p. 125; Harriet Hudson, *Four Middle English Romances,* TEAMS, available online; George Shuffleton, *Codex Ashmole 61: A Compilation of Popular Middle English Verse,* TEAMS, available online
Notes: Isumbras, reminded that his success is due to God, suffers Job-like misfortunes but in the end triumphs and is restored

75. **Sir Landevale**
    DIMEV #5002
    Format: 538 lines, couplets
    Copies of English version: 1 MS., Bodleian Library MS. Rawlinson C.86
    Original Source: derived from Marie of France's *Lai de Lanval*
    Notes: a probable source for *Sir Launfal*

76. ***Sir Otuel/Otuel a Knight**
    DIMEV #1784
    Format: 1671 lines, couplets; defective at end
    Copies of English version: 2 MSS, but the second, Bodleian Douce 376, is a copy of *Auchinleck MS/Advocates 19.2.1
    Modern Editions: Nicolson, p. 31
    Notes: Cf. "Roland and Otuel," a second English translation of the same Charlemagne/Roland-themed original

77. **Sir Percyvell of Gales**
    DIMEV #3074
    Format: 2288 lines, modified 16-line tail rhyme with the form *aaabcccbdddbeeeb*
    Copies of English version: 1 MS., Lincoln Cathedral Library MS. 91, the Thornton MS.
    Modern Editions: Mills, *Ywain and Gawain*, p. 103; Mary Flowers Braswell, *Four Middle English Romances*, TEAMS, available online.
    Notes: An Arthurian story of Percival, with the story of his obscure birth but without the grail legend; Gawain is prominent.

78. **Sir Thopas** (by Geoffrey Chaucer)
    DIMEV #3097
    Format: 206 lines, 6-line tail rhyme
    Modern Editions: Chaucer/Benson, p. 213
    Notes: A parody of romances rather than a romance itself, and incomplete, but it is a very deliberate example of the *form*, if not the content, of romances.

79. **Sir Torrent of Portyngale**
    DIMEV #1608
    Format: 2669 lines, 12-line tail rhyme
    Copies of English version: 1 MS, Manchester, Chetham 8009, very badly copied, plus 2 print fragments
    Modern Editions: Erich Adam, *Torrent of Portyngale*, Early English Text Society, 1887, available on Project Gutenberg
    Notes: Early fifteenth century. Probably influenced by the earlier *Sir Eglamore of Artois*. It is said to have a "strong ecclesiastical bias." The state of the manuscript has led some scholars to believe that it was taken from recitation.[195]

80. ***Sir Tristrem**
    DIMEV #2305
    Format: 3511 lines, 11-line stanzas, rhymed *abababaabcbc*, with the ninth line being only one foot long
    Copies of English version: 1 MS, *Auchinleck MS/Advocates 19.2.1

Modern Editions: Alan Lupack, *Lancelot of the Laik and Sir Tristrem,* TEAMS, available online
Notes: A version of the Tristan legend (the love interest is "Ysonde"), but with details not generally found in *Tristan* romances.

81. **†Sir Tryamoure**
    DIMEV #1924
    Format: 1719 lines, 12-line tail rhyme. The Percy folio version has 1539 lines.
    Copies of English version: 2 extant MSS and 1 now missing plus 1 complete print and two fragments]
    Modern Editions: Harriet Hudson, *Four Middle English Romances,* TEAMS, available online
    Notes: A tale of a young knight who defeats older challengers and marries into royalty, unrelated to the major romance cycles

82. **The Squire's Tale** (by Geoffrey Chaucer)
    DIMEV #725
    Format: 664 lines, couplets
    Modern Editions: Chaucer/Benson, p. 169
    Notes: Apparently an original romance to Chaucer—if it is a romance. It has no ending (possibly it, like *Sir Thopas,* was intended to be interrupted?), and the links are brief, plus some moderns see it as a satirical tale or a way of pointing up its teller's youth.[196]

83. **The Sultan of Babylon (The Sowdone of Babylone)**
    DIMEV #1562
    Format: 3274, quatrains rhymed *abab*
    Copies of English version: 1 MS., Princeton, Garrett 140
    Original Source: Probably paraphrased from a French original
    Modern Editions: Alan Lupack, *Three Middle English Charlemagne Romances,* TEAMS, available online
    Notes: A romance of Charlemagne, Roland, and Oliver, with many battles, ending with the obligatory conversion of various heathens

84. **The Tale of Beryn**
    DIMEV #6270
    Format: 3290 lines, couplets
    Copies of English version: 1 MS, Northumberland MS 455; an insertion in a rewritten text of the *Canterbury Tales,* sometimes called the "Merchant's Second Tale"
    Original Source: French romance, *Bérinus*
    Modern Editions: John M. Bowers, *The Canterbury Tales: Fifteenth-Century Continuations and Additions,* TEAMS, available online
    Notes: A tale of a nobleman who decides instead to be a merchant, and has to survive obstacles along the way; it is unrelated to the major romance cycles. Although the Northumberland MS. rewrites the *Canterbury Tales,* this is the only new tale, and probably predates the rewriting. It may well come from the period when "mass audience" romances, such as *Gamelyn* and the Robin Hood tales, were being written.

85. **The Tournament of Tottenham**
   DIMEV #4143
   Format: 234 lines, modified tail rhyme with very short lines and extra rhymed lines
   Copies of English version: 3 MSS.
   Modern Editions: Sands, p. 313; Erik Kooper, *Sentimental and Humorous Romances*, TEAMS, available online
   Notes: A parody of the romance genre, involving non-noble characters competing for a woman of similar station.

86. †**The Turke and Gawain**
   DIMEV #3096
   Format: 337 extant lines, 6-line tail rhyme; about half the original material missing
   Copies of English version: 1 MS, the †*Percy Folio*
   Modern Editions: Hahn, p. 337
   Notes: Northern dialect. Some features seem almost like a compilation of other romances.

87. **The Wars of Alexander**
   DIMEV #6306
   Format: 5677 lines extant, alliterative; ending lost
   Copies of English version: 2 MSS, both defective
   Original Source: based on Latin *Historia de Preliis*
   Modern Editions: Walter W. Skeat, *The Wars of Alexander: An Alliterative Romance, translated chiefly from the Historia Alexandri Magni de Preliis*, Early English Text Society, 1886, p. 1

88. **William of Palerne**
   DIMEV #5149
   Format: 1249 lines extant; alliterative; beginning and ending lost
   Copies of English version: 1 MS, Cambridge, King's College 13
   Original Source: French original, *Guillaume de Palerne*, which it follows closely; probably translated *c.* 1350
   Modern Editions: Walter W. Skeat, *William of Palerne, or William and the Werwolf*, p. 1

89. **Ywain and Gawain**
   DIMEV #439
   Format: 4032 lines, couplets
   Copies of English version: 1 MS., BL Cotton Galba E.ix
   Original Source: French original, *Le Chevalier au Lion*, by Chrétien de Troyes
   Modern Editions: Mills, *Ywain and Gawain*, p. 1; Mary Flowers Braswell, *Four Middle English Romances*, TEAMS, available online

Items mentioned in *The Complaynt of Scotlande* which might be part of a ballad-and-romance pair:

- *The tail quhou the king of esmure land mariet the kyngis dochtir of vestmure land* = King Estmere [Child 60]. This is a particularly interesting

situation, since "King Estmere," like "King Orfeo," is a tale of a king taking on the role of a minstrel.
- *The tail of Syr valtir, the bald Leslye* = Walter Lesly [Child 296] ?

We might also note significant similarities of theme between, e.g., Chaucer's *The Clerk's Tale* and both "Fair Annie" [Child 62] and "Child Waters" [Child 63].

## APPENDIX II
# *Manuscripts Containing ME Romances*

This is a partial list.[197] The names of the items have been standardized. No attempt is made to list manuscripts of *The Canterbury Tales*, either with or without copies of *Gamelyn*. That is listed for manuscripts which contain it and other romances (it can be assumed that these also contain other parts of *The Canterbury Tales*).

A brief summary of other items in the manuscript follows the list of romances. If the other items appear to include ballads, the manuscript is marked in **bold**. Of the 89 manuscripts listed, I would consider only ten to have ballad-like material, but these ten include some of the most important of all romance MSS: Ashmole 61, BL Add 27879 (the *Percy Folio*), BL Add 31042 (the London Thornton MS), BL Harley 2253 (the "Harley Lyrics"), Cambridge University Ee.4.35 (Richard Calle's MS.), and Balliol 354 (the Richard Hill MS.). Without these mixed manuscripts, our knowledge of the romances would be much less—fully a tenth of them would be completely lost (i.e. *The Carle of Carlisle, The Greene Knight, Ipomedon A, Robin Hood and the Monk, Robin Hood and the Potter, Roland and Otuel, The Sege of Melayne, Sir Gawain and the Carle of Carlisle, Sir Torrent of Portyngale, The Turke and Gawain*), and our knowledge of many others would be much reduced. Of the roughly 180 manuscript instances of romances other than Chaucer and Gower, the miscellanies account for 33.

Note that several romances, including *The Geste of Robyn Hode*, survive only in printed copies; these are not listed below, since printers had different criteria for what they printed; they tended to avoid miscellanies.

Badminton, Duke of Beaufort MN 704.1.16: *Richard Coeur de Lion [incomplete]*
Bodleian Library MS. Ashmole 33, late XIV, badly faded: *Sir Firumbras*
Bodleian Library MS. Ashmole 44, late XV: *The Wars of Alexander*
Bodleian Library MS. Ashmole 45 (6926), XVI: *The Erle of Tolous, Gamelyn* (also a part of Chaucer's *Cook's Tale*, a translation of Vegetius's *De Re Militari*, and some religious verse)

**Bodleian Library MS. Ashmole 61 (6922), XV, copied by a scribe named Rate:**[198] *The Erle of Tolous, Libeaus Desconus, Sir Cleges, Sir Isumbras, Sir Orfeo;* also *King Edward and the Hermit* [fragment] (also saints' lives, some material from Lydgate, religious verse, "The Debate of the Carpenter's Tools," miracle tales, "The Cucwold's Daunce," a story of an incestuous daughter, and "The Adulterous Falmouth Squire")

Bodleian Library MS. Douce 124 (transcription of Auchinleck; no independent value): *Arthour and Merlin [incomplete]*

Bodleian Library MS. Douce 216 (early XV): *Apollonius of Tyre* [fragments]

Bodleian Library MS Douce 228: *Richard Coeur de Lion [partial]*

Bodleian Library MS. Douce 236, late XV: *Arthour and Merlin*

Bodleian Library MS. Douce 261 (Bodleian 21835), 1564: *The Jeaste of Sir Gawain* [copied from print], *Sir Degaré* [fragments], *Sir Eglamore of Artois, Sir Isumbras*

Bodleian Library MS. Douce 309: *The Anturs of Arther*

Bodleian Library MS. Douce 324 (Bodleian 21898), late XV: *The Anturs of Arther*

Bodleian Library MS. Douce 326 (Bodleian 21900), c. 1400: *Amis and Amiloun* (also a short "Envoy addressed to Our Lady")

Bodleian Library MS. Douce 376 (transcription of Auchinleck; no independent value): *Sir Otuel*

Bodleian Library MS. Eng. Poet. a.1 (Bodleian 3938, the Vernon MS),[199] c. 1400: *Joseph of Arimathea, The King of Tars, A Pistil of Susan, Robert of Sicily* (also much of the *South English Legendary,* including many saints' lives; material from the *Golden Legend* and other religious materials [much of it entirely non-historical]; plus more than 300 prayers, gospel tales, exempla, homilies, and psalm texts; Miracles of the Virgin, a copy of the "A" text of *Piers Plowman,* and poems of Laurence Minot. There is a verse telling of the story of Esther which approaced the status of a romance.)

Bodleian Library MS. Eng. Poet. c.3: *Partonope of Blois [fragment]* (also several gospels and homilies as well as the Legend of Ipotis)

Bodleian Library MS. Latin Misc. b.17 (2 leaves only): *Partonope of Blois* [fragment] (also three gospel texts and a homily)

Bodleian Library MS. Laud Misc. 108, c. 1400: *King Horn, Havelok the Dane* (also many saints' lives from the *South English Legendary,* a poetic [and apocryphal] history of the infancy, "The disputation between the body and the soul," and "Somer Soneday")

Bodleian Library MS. Laud Misc. 622: *King Alisaunder* (also the Life of St. Alexis, Adam Davy's dreams of Edward II, some religious pieces, and "The Destruction of Jerusalem")

Bodleian Library MS. Rawlinson C.86 (Bodleian 11951), XV/XVI:[200] *Sir Landevale, The Wedding of Sir Gawain and Dame Ragnell* (also "The Friar and the Boy," many religious aphorisms and short lyrics, as well as longer poems, some Lydgate, several pieces mixing Latin and English, portions of the *Canterbury Tales* [out of order], *The Tale of Guiscardo and Ghismonda,* and metrical information about the Kings of England*)*

Bodleian Library MS. Rawlinson poet F.34: *Sir Degaré* (also saints' lives and passions and other religious poems)

Bodleian Library MS. Rawlinson Poet. 14: *Partonope of Blois [incomplete]*

Bodleian Library MS. Rawlinson Poet. 175 (Bodleian 14667), *c.* 1350: *The Seven Sages of Rome {DIMEV #3187}* (also much religious material.)

British Library, Additional MS. 22283, *c.* 1400 (the Simeon MS): *The King of Tars, Robert of Sicily [incomplete], A Pistil of Susan* (also dozens of gospel readings and items from the *Northern Homily Cycle* plus the *Legend of Ypotis,* religious lyrics, a translation of Grosseteste, and a few lyrics on events of the period 1377-1382)

**British Library, Additional MS. 27879 (*The Percy Folio*), *c.* 1650: *Arthour and Merlin, Eger and Grime, The Greene Knight, Libeaus Desconus, The Turke and Gawain, Sir Eglamore of Artois, Sir Tryamore, The Carle of Carlisle, Sir Degaré, Sir Tryamore, [short form of] The Squire of Low Degree, [short form of] Sir Landevale; two short forms of Guy of Warwick romances [Guy & Phyllis and Guy & Colbrande]* (also King Arthur and King Cornwall, The Marriage of Sir Gawain, Robin Hood and Guy of Gisburn, and many ballads)**

British Library, Additional MS 31042 (Robert Thornton MS, the "London Thornton MS"; cf. Lincoln Cathedral Library MS. A.5.2 (91), the Lincoln Thornton MS.), *c.* 1440: *Richard Coeur de Lion [partial], Roland and Otuel, The Sege of Melayne* (also several carols and ballad-like pieces, as well as *The Siege of Jerusalem* and other religious poetry, plus a prose rendering of the *Wars of Alexander*); see. J. J. Thompson, *The London Thornton Manuscript*

British Library, Additional MS. 34801, *c.* 1425: *Robert of Sicily [fragment]*

British Library, Additional MS. 35288: *Partonope of Blois [incomplete]*

British Library, MS. Arundel 140, XV: *The Seven Sages of Rome {DIMEV #4984}* (also a short item, in couplets, on Guy of Warwick)

British Library, MS. Cotton Caligula A.II: *Chevelere Assigne, Emaré, Libeaus Desconus, Octavian 2, Sir Eglamore of Artois, Sir Isumbras, Sir Launfal, A Pistil of Susan* (also several poems by Lydgate, an elegy for Lord Cromwell, *The Sege of Jerusalem,* and much religious poetry)

British Library, MS. Cotton Galba E.ix (early XV): *The Seven Sages of Rome {DIMEV #3187}, Ywain and Gawain* (also many works of Laurence Minot plus other historical poems, a few religious works, the Prophecy of Merlin, and *The Pricke of Conscience*)

British Library, MS. Cotton Nero A.x: *Sir Gawain and the Green Knight* (also *Pearl, Cleanness, Patience*, and a single-couplet lover's lament)

British Library, MS. Cotton Vitellius D.iii (c. 1300): *Floris and Blancheflour*

British Library, MS. Egerton 1995, late XV: *The Seven Sages of Rome {DIMEV #4984}* (also several poems on sports, plus a few proverbs and history poems)

British Library, MS. Egerton 2862, late XIV: *Amis and Amiloun, Bevis of Hampton, Floris and Blancheflour, Richard Coeur de Lion [partial], Sir Degaré* [fragment], *Sir Eglamore of Artois* (also a piece on the Fall of Troy)

British Library, MS. Harley 525, late XV: *Robert of Sicily [partial]* (also *The Siege of Troy* and *Speculum Gyde Warewyke*)

British Library, MS. Harley 1701, late XIV: *Robert of Sicily [partial]* (also *Handlyng Synne* and another religious poem by Robert of Brunne)

British Library, MS. Harley 2252, (two scribes, perhaps late XIV and mid XVI?): *Ipomedon B, The Stanzaic Morte Arthur* (also poems by Skelton and Lydgate, proverbs, wisdom poems, poetry on wine, a goodnight by the Third Duke of Buckingham, two pieces regarding Flodden, a prayer for Henry VIII, and more)

**British Library, MS. Harley 2253, *c.* 1330 (source of the famous "Harley Lyrics"): *King Horn* (also *The Song of Lewes, The Song of the Husbandman*, love lyrics including the famous *Alysoun*, and many religious and love pieces as well as some historical and instructional items)**

British Library, MS. Harley 2386, *c.* 1500: *Amis and Amiloun*

British Library, MS. Harley 3810, XV: *Sir Orfeo* (also *The Lady Who Buried the Host*, a love letter, and religious works)

British Library, MS Harley 4690, mutilated at beginning and end: *Richard Coeur de Lion [fragment]* (also a short item on the Battle of Halidon Hill)

**British Library, MS. Harley 5396, *The Tournament of Tottenham* (also *The Adulterous Falmouth Squire* and many religious pieces including carols)**

British Library, MS Harley 6223, mid-XVI, written by John Stow: *Arthour and Merlin*

British Library, MS Royal 17.B.43: *Sir Gowther* (plus two short religious poems)

British Library, MS Sloane 1044: *Guy of Warwick A* (also the *Pricke of Conscience*)

Cambridge, Emmanuel College MS. 405: *Generides B [fragments]*

Cambridge, Gonville and Caius College MS. 107/176: *Guy of Warwick A*

Cambridge, Gonville and Caius College MS. 174/95, late XV: *Robert of Sicily* (also *Sir Peny* and several religious works)

Cambridge, Gonville and Caius College MS. 175, c. 1500:[201] *Athelston, Bevis of Hampton, Richard Coeur de Lion [partial], Sir Isumbras* (also the life of St. Katherine and the hours of the Cross)

Cambridge, King's College MS 13: *William of Palerne* (also many segments of the South English Legendary)

Cambridge, Trinity College Library MS. O.5.2, XV:[202] *Generides B [incomplete]* (also the *Troy Book*, Lydgate's *Siege of Thebes*, and some short poems)

Cambridge University Library MS. Dd.1.17, late XIV: *The Seven Sages of Rome {DIMEV #4986}* (also the "B" text of *Piers Plowman*)

**Cambridge University Library MS. Ee.4.35 (Richard Calle's MS):[203] *Robin Hood and the Potter, The King and the Barker* [i.e. *King Edward and the Shepherd*] (also *The Adulterous Falmouth Squire, The Friar and the Boy*, and some educational rhymes)**

Cambridge University Library MS. Ff.i.6 (made by and for the Findern family of Derbyshire, c. 1450)[204]: *Sir Degrevant* (also the *Confessio Amantis*, the *Parlement of Foules, The Legend of Good Women*, and other Chaucer poems, much love poetry, and some miscellaneous verse)

Cambridge University Library MS. Ff.2.38, late XV[205]: *Bevis of Hampton, Le Bone Florence of Rome, The Erle of Tolous, Guy of Warwick B, Octavian 1, Robert of Sicily, The Seven Sages of Rome {DIMEV #4984}, Sir Degaré* [fragments], *Sir Eglamore of Artois, Sir Triamour* (also much metrical religious material such as saints' lives, plus *The Adulterous Falmouth Squire*, and a dirty stanza, with the religious material at the beginning and the romances at the end)

**Cambridge University Library MS. Ff.5.48, late XV, with at least one text based on the writing of Gilbert Pilkington:[206] *King Edward and the Shepherd, The Tournament of Tottenham, Robin Hood and the Monk* (plus much religious material, some of it in Latin; several items are labelled "ballads" e.g. "A ballad on an incontinent priest," "Another ballad on the provisions at a feast"; also *The Adulterous Falmouth Squire*)**

Cambridge University Library MS. Gg. 4.27.2, c. 1500:[207] *Floris and Blancheflour, King Horn* (also many works of Chaucer, Henryson's *Testament of Cresseid*, a lament for Edward IV, and some short poems)

Cambridge University Library MS. Ii.4.9, late XV: *Robert of Sicily*

Cambridge University Library MS. Kk.1.5, c. 1500: *Lancelot of the Laik* (also some religious poems and maxims)

Cambridge University Library Add. 4407: *Havelock the Dane* [fragments] (also a fragment of a religious poem)

Cambridge (Mass.), Harvard University, Houghton Library MS English 530: *The Tournament of Tottenham* (also several short pieces from the Scots wars and two long poems by Lychefelde and Lydgate)

Dublin, Trinity College MS. 213 D, late XV: *The Wars of Alexander* (also the "A" text of *Piers Plowman*)

Dublin, Trinity College MS. 432 B, c. 1465: *Robert of Sicily* (also much material on the Yorkist faction in the Wars of the Roses, a play on Abraham and Isaac, some wisdom material, and some religious material, some of it ballad-like)

Glasgow University Library MS. Hunterian V.2.8 (388) [c. 1540; copied by Thomas Chetham of Nuthurst, Lancashire]: *The Destruction of Troy*

Huntington HM 114 (Phillips 8252), mid-XV: *A Pistil of Susan* (also the "B" text of *Piers Plowman* and *Troilus and Criseyde*)

Lambeth Palace Library (London), MS. 491, XV?: *The Anturs of Arther* (also *The Sege of Jerusalem*, a book on hunting, and several religious works)

Lincoln Cathedral Library MS. A.5.2 (91) (the Lincoln Thornton MS, copied in part by Robert Thornton; cf. British Library, Additional MS 31042, the "London Thornton MS"), c. 1440: *The Erle of Tolous, The Alliterative Morte Arthure, Octavian 1, Sir Degrevant [lacks 1 page], Sir Eglamore of Artois, Sir Isumbras, Sir Percyvell of Gales, The Anturs of Arther* (also saints' lives, *Thomas of Ercildoune's Prophecy*, several prayers and religious poems, and *The Pricke of Conscience*)

**London, College of Arms MS Arundel 58: *Richard Coeur de Lion* [fullest known copy, but incomplete, with some prose portions] (also Robert of Gloucester's Chronicle, a poetic list of English kings, and ballad-like poem on the Battle of Halidon Hill)**

London, Gray's Inn MS 20 (mid-XIV): *Sir Isumbras* {fragment} (also a poetic legend of Saint Anastasia)

London, Lincoln's Inn Library MS 150, XIV and XV: *Arthour and Merlin* (part), *King Alisaunder, Libeaus Desconus* (also *The Siege of Troy* and an "A" text of *Piers Plowman*)

**Manchester MS. Chetham 8009, late XV: *Bevis of Hampton, Ipomedon A, Sir Torrent of Portyngale* (also several religious works, a book on social behavior, and a "Ballad of a tyrannical husband")**

Naples, Bibliotheca Nazionale MS XIII B.29: *Bevis of Hampton, Libeaus Desconus, Sir Isumbras [fragment]*, plus Chaucer's *Clerk's Tale* (also some minor religious/sententious poetry)

National Library of Scotland MS. 16500 (the Asloan MS): *The Seven Sages of Rome {DIMEV #4987}* (also much poetry of Dunbar, Henryson, and others)

National Library of Scotland, Advocates MS. 19.1.11, c. 1400: *Sir Cleges* (also "Erthe upon Erthe," and some religious material)

National Library of Scotland, Advocates MS. 19.2.1 (the Auchinleck MS), early XIV: *Amis and Amiloun, Arthour and Merlin, Bevis of Hampton, Floris and Blancheflour, Guy of Warwick A (and additional Guy material), Horn Childe and Maiden Rimnild, King Alisaunder, The King of Tars, Lay le Freine, Reinbroun, Richard Coeur de Lion [fragment], Roland and Vernagu, The Seven Sages of Rome {DIMEV #4984}, Sir Degaré, Sir Orfeo, Sir Otuel, Sir Tristrem* (also *The Thrush and the Nightingale* plus several saints' lives and other religious material such as *The Assumption of the Virgin*, a political piece about the Magna Carta, and other historical works)

National Library of Scotland, Advocates MS. 19.3.1 (Jac V.7.27, the "Heege" MS.), late XV: *Sir Amadace, Sir Gowther, Sir Isumbras* (also *The Hunting of the Hare*, some nonsense lyrics, and religious lyrics, including the carol "This Endris Night")

**National Library of Wales (Aberystwyth), MS. Porkington 10, XV: Sir Gawain and the Carle of Carlisle (also *The Friar and the Boy*, several love poems, some religious works, assorted carols, *The Ten Wives Tales*, and a weather prognostication)**

Northumberland MS. 455, late XV: *The Tale of Beryn* (also the *Canterbury Tales*)

**Oxford, Balliol College 354 (the Richard Hill MS.), early XVI: Confessio Amantis, The Seven Sages of Rome {DIMEV #4984} (also *The Friar and the Boy*, some informative poems, historical materials, proverbs, some religious material, and many carols)**[208]

Oxford, Trinity College 57, late XV: *Robert of Sicily* (also many saints' lives and other religious material)

Oxford, University College 142, late XIV: *Sir Isumbras* [fragment] (also *The Pricke of Conscience* and an Easter poem)

Oxford, University College 188: *Partonope of Blois [incomplete]*

Pierpont Morgan Library MS. M 818 (Ingilby MS), mid-XV: *A Pistil of Susan* (also the "A" text of *Piers Plowman*, a part of the "B" text, and a few short religious items)

Pierpont Morgan Library MS. M876: *Generides A* (also the *Troy Book*)

Princeton, Garrett 140 (mid XV): *The Sultan of Babylon*

Princeton, Garrett 141 (late XV): *Amoryus and Cleopes*

Princeton, Robert H. Taylor collection, Ireland Blackburn MS, late XV: *The Anturs of Arther, Sir Amadace, The Avowying of Arthur*

Tokyo, Takamiya MS 32 (formely Penrose 6): *Partonope of Blois [fragment] [sole copy of the version listed as DIMEV #6533], Gamelyn* (plus *The Adulterous Falmouth Squire*, the *Confessio Amantis*, and much of *The Canterbury Tales*)

## ENDNOTES

[1] Francis James Child, *The English and Scottish Popular Ballads*, 10 volumes. (N.B. references are to volume and page in the five volume Dover edition), ballads #19, volume I, pp. 215-217; #17, volume I, pp. 187-208; and #300, volume V, pp. 175-176.

[2] Child #273, volume V, pp. 67-87.

[3] Child #30, volume I, pp. 274-288.

[4] Thomas Hahn, editor, *Sir Gawain: Eleven Romances and Tales*, TEAMS (Consortium for the Teaching of the Middle Ages), Medieval Institute Publications, Western Michigan University, 1995, pp. 419. Given that the surviving material is 300 lines, and represents only about half the total, the length certainly seems more typical of romances.

[5] Holger Olof Nygard, "Popular Ballad and Medieval Romance," originally from D. K. Wilgus, editor, *Folklore International: Essay in Honor of Wayland Debs Hand*, 1967; reprinted in E(mily) B. Lyle, *Ballad Studies*, Brewer/Roman and Littlefield, 1976. Citation is from the Lyle edition, p. 7, based on comments of Francis B. Gummere.

[6] Richard Garnett and Edmund Gosse, *English Literature: An Illustrated Record*, four volumes, MacMillan, 1903-1904 (references are to the 1935 MacMillan edition published in two volumes), volume I, p. 102.

[7] Old English samples of almost all of these can be found in Dorothy Whitelock, revisor, *Sweet's Anglo-Saxon Reader in Prose and Verse*, 15th edition, Oxford/Clarendon Press, 1967; for specimens in translation, see R. K. Gordon, *Anglo-Saxon Poetry*, 1926; revised edition, J. M. Dent, 1954.

[8] Roger Sherman Loomis and Laura Hibbard Loomis, editors and translators, *Medieval Romances*, 1957 (references are to the undated Modern Library paperback), p. vii.

[9] *Sir Gawain and the Green Knight*, translated by James L. Rosenberg, edited by and with an introduction by James L. Kreuzer, Holt, Rinehart and Winston, 1959; fifth printing, 1964, p. LII.

[10] W. P. Ker compared this to "the difference between the earlier 'heroic' age and the age of chivalry"; see W(illiam) P(aton) Ker, *Epic and Romance: Essays on Medieval Literature*, Macmillan and Co., 1897 (available on Google Books), p. 4.

[11] C. S. Lewis, *The Allegory of Love*, Oxford University Press, 1936 (references are to the 1958 paperback edition), p. 3, declares, "It seems to us natural that love should be the commonest theme of serious imaginative literature, but a glance at classical antiquity or at the Dark Ages at once shows us that what we took for 'nature' is really a special state of affairs... which certainly had a beginning in eleventh-century Provence." This is exaggerated. After all, the love stories of Orpheus and of Dido and Æneas are just some of the famous tales from the classics. Furthermore, Lewis over-stresses the

somewhat artificial construct known as "courtly love." Still, it is certainly true that the French romances put a new emphasis on love.

[12] Not everyone agrees that the Norman Conquest was a significant factor in the spread of romances in England. Sir A.W. Ward and A.R. Waller, editors, *The Cambridge History of English Literature,* Cambridge University Press, 1907 (references are to the 1967 reprint of the "cheap edition" of 1932), pp. 277-278, argues that the Conquest was not a major factor in the spread of romances because romances spread everywhere at about the same rate. Yet very many of the English romances were based on French originals; at minimum, the Norman Conquest meant that many more Englishmen were bilingual and understood the French romances.

[13] John Stevens, *Medieval Romance: Themes and Approaches,* 1973 (page references are to the 1974 Norton edition), p. 15.

[14] Loomis/Loomis, p. x.

[15] George K. Anderson, *Old and Middle English Literature from the Beginnings to 1485,* being volume I of "A History of English Literature," 1950 (references are to the 1966 Collier paperback edition), p. 84.

[16] Gawain/Rosenberg/Kreuzer, p. L.

[17] Gawain/Rosenberg/Kreuzer, p. LIV.

[18] Ward & Waller, p. 301.

[19] Lewis, p. 12.

[20] Stevens, p. 90, citing the values of the Knight from line 46 of the General Prologue of the *Canterbury Tales;* see Larry D. Benson, general editor, *The Riverside Chaucer,* third edition, Houghton Mifflin, 1987 (based on F. N. Robinson, *The Works of Geoffrey Chaucer,* which is considered to be the first and second editions of this work), p. 24.

[21] Ward & Waller, p. 318.

[22] Anderson, p. 84, referring specifically to Marie de France's *lais,* but the description applies to all the romances.

[23] Donald B. Sands, editor, *Middle English Verse Romances,* Holt, Rinehart and Winston, 1966., p. 130.

[24] J. A. W. Bennett, *Middle English Literature,* edited and completed by Douglas Gray and being a volume of the Oxford History of English Literature, 1986 (references are to the 1990 Clarendon paperback), p. 122.

[25] Bennett/Gray, p. 151.

[26] For *Tottenham* and *Gamelyn,* see Sands, pp. 313-322 and 154-181. For *Robyn* see now Robert B. Waltz, *The Gest of Robyn Hode,* Loomis House Press, 2012.

[27] Marie of France, *The Lais of Marie de France,* translated & introduced by Robert Hanning & Joan Ferrante, foreword by John Fowles, E. P. Dutton, 1978, p. 4.

[28] Stevens, p. 46.

[29] Stevens, p. 83, compares *Gamelyn* to a television Western, and the comparison has some truth. *Gamelyn* is one of the few romances where it is truly not obvious who is the "good guy;" we are supposed to sympathize with Gamelyn. Some might find him a brutal, stupid low-life.

[30] Stevens, pp. 97-98, with the order of the first and second sentences reversed. Tolkien in *The Hobbit* in particular makes this clear, with the "Tookish" half of Bilbo Baggins seeking adventures while the "Baggins" half seeks a regular schedule of meals and tea.

[31] Bennett/Gray, p. 126. Sometimes even a chivalrous romance could be based on a saint's life; Hahn, p. 169, and Ward/Waller, p. 312, declare that the first half of *The Awntyrs off Arthur* is based on material from the *Trentals of St. Gregory*.

[32] Stevens, p. 46.

[33] Northrup Frye, *Anatomy of Criticism*, 1957 (references are to the 2000 Princeton edition with a new foreword by Harold Bloom), p. 33. Frye on p. 50 gives an instance of how this operates by using ghosts as an example: "In romance we have real human beings, and consequently ghosts are a separate category, but in a romance a ghost as a rule is merely one more character."

[34] Stevens, p. 16.

[35] Stevens, p. 63, gives two examples from Chaucer—in the *Wife of Bath's Tale*, the question is "What do women want?" or "Who is to have sovereignty?"; in the Franklin's Tale it is, "Which is more important, fidelity to a spouse or fidelity to a promise?" and also "Who is most generous of spirit?"

[36] It is worth reminding ourselves that this was something of a new idea at the time. Lewis over-stressed Courtly Love, but his exposition on pp. 14-17 regarding the early Church's position on carnality is excellent. The church was very confused on the issue of passion within marriage—but those learned doctors and celibate bishops almost all condemned it to some degree. Even Paul (1 Corinthians 7:9) accepted sexual relations more by way of concession than anything else. It should also be remembered that Peter was married and that there was an early tradition that Jesus himself may have been married to Mary Magdalene. Only in the Middle Ages did passion start to be treated as a virtue in itself, and only then does it seem to have been regarded as related to Christian love (Stevens, p. 11). Note, e.g., the Prioress's emblem *amor vincit omnia* (Chaucer/Benson, p. 26, line 162); the Latin vulgate text of 1 Corinthians 13, from which the idea "love conquers all" derives, consistently uses the noun *caritas*, i.e. *charitable love*, not *amor*, i.e. *passionate love*. This confusion of religious and love themes is so strong that Stevens devotes a whole chapter (pp. 119-141) to "Man and God: Religion and Romance," much of it occupied with the way in which the romances combine religious imagery and ceremony with love themes.

[37] Stevens, pp. 64-65, defining the essence of the dilemma of Chaucer's *Franklin's Tale* (in many ways the most refined of all the Breton Lais); compare his comments on pp. 74-75 regarding *Yvain*. To be sure, Chaucer/Benson, pp. 895-896, notes that many scholars in recent years have attempted to find ulterior motives or a dark plot in the

*Franklin's Tale.* But even if these attacks are held to be a success, they do not change the basis of Chaucer's use of *trouthe;* they simply de-romanticize the *Franklin's Tale.*

[38] Stevens, p. 78.

[39] Anderson, p. 80

[40] Stevens, p. 28.

[41] Stevens, pp. 78-79.

[42] J. R. R. Tolkien, "On Fairy-stories," being the Andrew Lang lecture for 1938, published as an article in *Essays Presented to Charles Williams,* 1947; reprinted in *The Tolkien Reader,* Ballantine, 1966, p. 68. He considers this potential for success or failure to be the heart of the "fairy-story." It is also at the heart of the romance. Tolkien's own work, *The Lord of the Rings,* of course, shows this very clearly, as the world teeters on a knife's edge in the final section—and is saved only at great cost and by a seeming lucky accident.

[43] Marie de France's Breton Lais, which functionally define the genre, were apparently written in England, and even include occasional words in English; Marie de France, *The Lais of Marie de France,* translated and with an introduction by Glyn S. Burgess and Keith Busby, Penguin, 1986, p. 22. To be sure, Bennett/Gray, p. 139, refer to the Breton Lais as coming from Brittany, but the term seems primarily to refer to songs with strong Celtic—"Breton," i.e. "British"—influence.

[44] Some moderns defend the modern romances on the grounds of their similarity to the medieval romances. Stevens, p. 9, goes so far as to reverse that: He justifies study of medieval romances on the grounds of their similarity to modern romances, citing Tolkien in particular.

[45] Tom Shippey, *The Road to Middle-Earth,* Revised and Expanded Edition, Houghton Mifflin, 2003, p. 62, even speculates "that the 'master-text' for Tolkien's portrayal of the elves is the description of the hunting king in *Sir Orfeo.*" This list of parallels between Tolkien's works and *Sir Orfeo* could easily be extended—e.g. I personally see a bit of Orfeo's steward in Tolkien's Sam Gamgee, who is the servant of Frodo Baggins but, once Frodo departs, becomes a major figure in his own right and the long-time Mayor of the Shire.

[46] G. Blakemore Evans, textual editor, assisted by J. J. M. Tobin and others, *The Riverside Shakespeare,* Houghton Mifflin, 1974; second edition, Houghton Mifflin, 1977, p x, lists five Shakespeare plays as romances: *Pericles, Prince of Tyre; Cymbeline; The Winter's Tale, The Tempest;* and *The Two Noble Kinsmen.*

[47] This is the estimate of Sands (p. 56). The list in Appendix I of this book counts even more, but this includes multiple versions of some tales (e.g. *Ipomedon),* and while all these writings have been called romances by someone, few scholars would count all of them as such.

[48] Stephen Knight, "The Social Function of the Middle English Romance" (1986), as cited by William Fahrenbach, "Rereading Clement in Thomas Chestre's *Octavian* and BL Cotton Caligula A.II," *Essays in Medieval Studies,* Volume 26 (2010), pp. 85-86

[49] Sands, p. 56.

[50] Carl Lindahl, "The Oral Undertones of Late Medieval Romance," in W. F. H. Nicolaisen, editor, *Oral Tradition in the Middle Ages*, Medieval & Renaissance Texts & Studies, Volume 112, 1995, pp. 61-62.

[51] Sands, p. 56.

[52] Nygard, p. 19.

[53] Kurt Witting, *The Scottish Tradition in Literature*, Oliver and Boyd, 1958, p. 104.

[54] Anna Hunt Billings, *A Guide to the Middle English Metrical Romances, Dealing with English and Germanic Legends, and with the Cycles of Charlemagne and of Arthur*, Henry Holt and Company, 1901 (available on Google Books), pp. X-XI.

[55] Sands, p. 202, counts a total of 23 tail rhyme romances.

[56] Chaucer/Benson, p. 917

[57] Chaucer/Benson, fragment VII, lines 833-838 (*2023-2028), p. 215

[58] Billings, p. XI, quoting Brandl, but the form, as Billings admits, is of Latin origin and appears to have been more typical of church productions.

[59] Several examples in Thorlac Turville-Petre, *Alliterative Poetry of the Later Middle Ages: An Anthology*, Routledge, 1989, pp. 158-212. The alliterative line was hard to sing, but it had advantages for sound effects; Bennett/Gray, p. 132 note for instance that "romance writers… would mass plosives and sibilants together to evoke the noise of conflict." An excellent example of this comes from the opening of *Sir Gawain and the Green Knight*: "Siþen þe sege and þe assaut watz sesed at Troye"—"Since the siege and the assault was ceased at Troy. (J. R. R. Tolkien and E. V. Gordon, *Sir Gawain and the Green Knight*, second edition revised and edited by Norman Davis, Oxford, 1967, p. 1). Here the alternation of *th* and *s* is particularly effective, as it gives the impression of running and slowing down and attacking again.

[60] Tolkien/Gordon/Davis, pp. 147-152. On p. 152 they declare that no other poem has this exact structure, although there are others with similar bob-and-wheels.

[61] Sands, p. 156.

[62] Sands, p. 16, who notes however that the lines of "King Horn" are very short.

[63] Not explicitly noted in Sands, but see the text on pp. 282-309.

[64] Again, no explicit statement in Sands, but see pp. 251-278.

[65] Bennett/Gray, p. 139. It has been suggested that French romances were more often designed to be read, English more likely to be publicly performed.

[66] Benson, fragment V, lines 709-712, p. 178.

[67] Sands, p. 201.

[68] Maldwyn Mills, editor, *Six Middle English Romances*, Everyman's Library, 1973 (references are to the 1992 J. M. Dent paperback), pp. ix-x.

[69] Sands, p. 279; Child, volume V., p. 175.

⁷⁰ e.g. Ward & Waller, p. 327, on the basis that the tale says it had been "locked in lettered lore." But surely this means merely that portions of the Arthurian legend have been written down, not that *Sir Gawain* is a translation of a lost original!

⁷¹ Oskar Seyffert, *The Dictionary of Classical Mythology, Religion, Literature, and Art*, 1882; English edition 1891; revised and edited by Henry Nettleship and J. E. Sandys, Gramercy Books, 1995, p. 438.

⁷² Pierre Grimal, *The Penguin Dictionary of Classical Mythology*, based on Grimal's *Dictionnaire de la Mythologie Grecque et Romaine*, 1951, translated by A. R. Maxwell-Hyslop, 1986, edited and abridged by Stephen Kershaw, Penguin, 1990, p. 315.

⁷³ Grimal, p. 315.

⁷⁴ Grimal, p. 316.

⁷⁵ Michael Grant and John Hazel, *Gods and Mortals in Classical Mythology: A Dictionary*, 1973 (references are to the Dorset Press edition copyright 1979), p. 259.

⁷⁶ Based on Ovid [Publius Ovidius Naso], *Metamorphoses*, translated by Mary M. Innes, Penguin, 1955, pp. 225-227.

⁷⁷ Virgil [Publius Vergilius Maro], *Virgil I: Eclogues, Georgics, Aeneid I-VI* (Loeb edition, Latin and English), translated by H. Rushton Fairclough, revised edition, Loeb Classical Library, Harvard University Press, 1916, 1935, pp. 228-233; also Virgil [Publius Vergilius Maro], *Virgil's Works: The Aeneid, Eclogues, and Georgics*, translated by J. W. McKail with an introduction by William C. McDermott, Modern Library College Editions, 1950, pp. 349-351.

⁷⁸ Book 3, metre 12, according to J. A. Burrow and Thorlac Turville-Petre, *A Book of Middle English*, second edition, 1996 (references are to the 1999 Blackwell paperback edition), p. 112. Boethius doesn't really tell the tale; he just alludes to it; in Chaucer's prose translation of Boethius into Middle English prose (usually called "Boece"; see Chaucer/Benson, p. 439); it takes only about 70 lines. Chaucer in any case wrote after *Sir Orfeo* was completed—and although Boethius strongly influenced Chaucer, the philosopher's treatment of the Orpheus legend is as unromantic as it could possibly be; he treats it not as an excess of love but a failure of love (Chaucer/Benson, p. 396).

⁷⁹ Sands, p. 186.

⁸⁰ Marie de France/Hanning/Fernante, p. 4. Ovid's work was the basis for at least one other Middle English romance; John Metham's *Amoryus and Cleopes* is a clear adaption of the tale of Pyramus and Thisbe.

⁸¹ Grant/Hazel, p. 258.

⁸² Robert L. Kindrick, *The Poems of Robert Henryson*, TEAMS (Consortium for the Teaching of the Middle Ages), Medieval Institute Publications, Western Michigan University, 1997; now available at http://www.lib.rochester.edu/camelot/teams/orphint.htm. Site checked Nov. 22, 2012.

⁸³ Burrow/Turville-Petre, p. 113.

⁸⁴ Emily Lyle, *Fairies and Folk: Approaches to the Scottish Ballad Tradition*, Wissenschaflicher Verlag Trier, 2007, p. 71.

⁸⁵ Lyle, pp. 71-72. The *Recueil* bears the incidental distinction of being the first book printed in English; Caxton translated it and eventually published his translation.

⁸⁶ Lyle, p. 66; Burrow/Turville-Petre, p. 113; Loomis/Loomis, p. 312, refers to this *lai* being sung by an Irish harper.

⁸⁷ Sands, p. 185.

⁸⁸ H. S. Bennett, *Chaucer and the Fifteenth Century*, being Volume II, Part I of the *Oxford History of English Literature*, Oxford University Press, 1947, 1954, p. 11.

⁸⁹ Loomis/Loomis, pp. 311-312.

⁹⁰ Sisam, p. 13.

⁹¹ Burrow/Turville-Petre, p. 112.

⁹² Tolkien, *On Fairy Stories*, p. 9.

⁹³ Child, volume I, pp. 318-319.

⁹⁴ Thomas of Ercildoune of course was summoned to Faërie at the end of his life, and we also read that Wade, seemingly the hero of a lost romance, now dwells there; Bennett/Gray, p. 125.

J. R. R. Tolkien, who probably studied the subject more than any other modern scholar, seems to have felt that Faërie was a place of high peril but essentially good. In his Middle-Earth, Mordor seems to have been the true hell, with Lórien very likely the equivalent of Faërie. Of Lórien Aragorn says (here speaking with what seems to be Tolkien's own voice) that it is "fair and perilous, but only evil need fear it, or those who bring some evil with them" (J. R. R. Tolkien, *The Lord of the Rings, volume I: The Fellowship of the Ring*, second edition, Houghton Mifflin, 1965, p. 253). The matter is even more explicit in *Smith of Wooton Major*, in which Smith, like Orfeo, actually travels from our world to "Faery." Smith has to be protected from the strange and wild land, but he is made better by his presence—and, in the tale, the King of Faërie plays a Christ-like role, coming among humanity in humble guise (Tolkien, *Smith of Wooton Major and Farmer Giles of Ham*, Nelson Doubleday, 1967, 1975, 1976, pp. 28-34).

⁹⁵ Stevens, p. 87, notes that even Beroul's version of the Tristan legend, usually treated as a pure tale of love, is in fact primarily a tale of loyalty.

⁹⁶ Bennett/Gray, p. 140.

⁹⁷ Loomis/Loomis, p. 313.

⁹⁸ Kenneth Sisam, editor, *Fourteenth Century Verse & Prose* (with a Middle English vocabulary by J. R. R. Tolkien), Oxford at the Clarendon Press, 1925, p. 13, referring to his lines 49-50

⁹⁹ The romance is *Guy of Warwick*. Lyle, pp. 67-70; she thinks *Sir Orfeo* likely borrowed this part of the tale from *Guy*. Obviously this is possible, but the defect with this supposition is that the abduction and rescue is not an inherent part of *Guy*, whereas Orpheus isn't Orpheus without the journey to the other world. It makes more sense

to assume Orpheus was transformed to Orfeo and the legend then borrowed. Lyle, p. 72, also notes a similarity to one version of the Tristan legend, but this is not a general part of that legend.

[100] National Library of Scotland MS. Advocates 19.2.1. A transcription of the manuscript, with photographs, can be found at the site *The Auchinleck Manuscript*, eds David Burnley and Alison Wiggins, by the National Library of Scotland, July 5, 2003, version 1.1, at http:// auchinleck.nls.uk/. The manuscript itself is at http://auchinleck.nls.uk/mss/orfeo.html. Site checked September 3, 2012.

[101] Exceptions are A. J. Bliss, *Sir Orfeo*, Oxford, 1954, which prints all three manuscripts; George Shuffleton, *Codex Ashmole 61: A Compilation of Popular Middle English Verse*, Medieval University Press/TEAMS, 2008, which works from Ashmole; Joseph Ritson, *Ancient English Metrical Romances*, 1802, reprinted by Goldsmid, 1885, which works fro Harley; and Rumble, *op. cit.*, based on Ashmole.

[102] Sisam, p. 13.

[103] Sisam, pp. 14-31. This should not be taken as an endorsement of this text; indeed, it seems to me that *Sir Orfeo* needs a thorough re-editing. It appears, based on an admittedly-casual examination of the texts, that the stemma of the three manuscripts is as follows, with the length of the branches showing the amount of variation from the archetype:

```
                    α ┬── Auchinleck
Archetype ┬─────────┤
          │         └── γ ──────── Harley
          │
          └── β ──────────────────── Ashmole
```

Ashmole in particular shows signs of having gone through an oral transmission phase. This argues strongly for a more eclectic approach to the text rather than simply adopting Auchinleck or Ashmole as a copy-text. For purposes of historical comparison, however, simply choosing a text is probably sufficient. And Sisam's text is probably the most accessible, since it is the one associated with J. R. R. Tolkien's modernization. The text has been compared against Burrow/Turville-Petre, pp. 114-131; Anne Laskaya and Eve Salisbury, *Sir Orfeo*, from *The Middle English Breton Lays*, originally published by Medieval Institute Publications, 1995 and now available at http://www.lib.rochester.edu/camelot/teams/orfeofrm.htm; site checked September 14-26, 2012; Thomas C. Rumble, editor, *The Breton Lays in Middle English*, 1964 (references are to the 1967 Wayne State University paperback edition which corrects a few errors in the original printing), pp. 207-226 ("Kyng Orfew," a version based on Ashmole 61 rather than Auchinleck and as a result very different); and Sands, pp. 187-200, who however omits the prefatory lines. Reference has also been made to the modern verse edition by Tolkien (published as J. R. R. Tolkien, *Sir Gawain and the Green Knight/Pearl/Sir Orfeo*, Allen & Unwin, 1975; references are to the 1980 Ballantine paperback edition). Variant readings have been derived from Oscar Zielke, *Sir Orfeo: Ein Englisches Feenmärchen Aus dem Mittelalter*, Wilhelm Koebner, 1880, available on Google Books.

[104] *war:* Burrow/Turville-Petre and Laskaya/Salisbury give ME *"wer," war* (Rumble has "werre"); Zielke, Sisam, and apparently Tolkien and Loomis/Loomis *"wele," weal, prosperity*. "Wele" is the reading of Harley; Ashmole reads "werre;" according to Sands, p. 235, the *Lai Le Freine* also reads "werre." "War" former is perhaps slightly preferable as it contrasts two woes in line five with two joys in line six.

[105] *Faërie:* ME *fayré* according to Sisam following Harley, *fairy* in Burrow/Turville-Petre and Laskaya/Salisbury, *fary* in Rumble (following Ashmole's reading "off fary"). Chaucer/Benson, p. 116, spells it "fayerye" in the *Wife of Bath's Tale*. There is little doubt that the name means *the fay land* or *the land of the feys (fates)*. "Faërie" is J. R. R. Tolkien's usage, and perhaps a hypertranslation, but it emphasizes the alienness and power of the other land. The word is certainly to be connected with magic.

[106] *Glee:* there seems to be no good modern equivalent of the medieval word "glee," and so I have necessarily retained it even though it now gives the false impression of a sort of manic happiness. In *Sir Orfeo* it refers to minstrelsy, or entertainment; a gleeman was an entertainer who could supply music, tales, and perhaps other amusements. The word can also refer to "mirth, joy, pleasure," but typically it is the more somber joy of a tale well told or a song well played.

[107] The text of this sentence is very uncertain and has been read in different ways by the editions. This version is closest to Burrow/Turville-Petrie, as it seemed to make the best sense.

[108] The order of lines 33-46 varies; they are not in the Auchinleck manuscript, and editors have differed on their location. This text follows Sisam, p. 15; Laskaya/Salisbury and Burrow/Turville-Petre place them after line 24.

[109] MSS. *Traciens/Tracyens*, generally understood to be Thrace in Greece. The link to Winchester was probably intended to compliment some local Winchester resident—a thirteenth or fourteenth Bishop of Winchester is a likely candidate, since the Winchester bishopric was very wealthy and the bishop would be a highly desirable patron. The sentence equating Thrace with Winchester is found only in Auchinleck; Thrace is mentioned in the other texts but not the English city.

[110] Herodis=Euridice. According to Zielke, p. 88, "Heurodis" is the reading of Auchinleck; Ashmole has "Meroudis" (this is probably an error of hearing or copying in the Ashmole MS); Harley reads "Erodys." The editions also differ in spelling; Rumble, following Ashmole, consistently reads "Meroudys"; Sisam uses "Herodis" here (although "Heurodis" in line 63), Sands gives "Herodis," Laskaya/Salisbury and Burrow/Turville-Petre emend to "Heurodis," which is also the spelling used by Tolkien. The latter of course is more reminiscent of "Euridice"—especially since the name is originally Greek and classical Greek did not have a symbol for the H sound; "Euridice" and "Heuridice" would have been spelled the same.

[111] According to Zielke, p. 89, Auchinleck and Harley read here a "ympetre," "ympe tre(e)"; Ashmole has "hympe tre(e)." The word "ympe," "impe," is rare but often means a shoot or seedling. Here, it is believed to refer to a grafted apple tree—a shoot which replaces a limb on a different tree. A grafted tree is a place where two different trees are

in contact, and hence presumably represents a place where two different worlds — our world and Faërie — also have close contact. Thus it is a place where the otherworld folk have access to ours.

It is interesting to note that another romance in the Auchinleck manuscript, *Sir Degaré*, involves a princess under a tree who is ravaged by a fairy knight (Bennett/Gray, p. 153).

[112] For these two lines Ashmole (and hence Rumble) has "And ever þou ast be meke and myld, Þou arte becom wode and wyld" — "And ever you have been meek and mild, you are become mad and wild."

[113] Rumble's version of these lines, slightly modernized, runs:
*Where thou art, I will be with thee,*
*And where I am, thou shall be with me!*
The version translated, however, is from Auchinleck:
*Whither thou goest, I will with thee,*
*And whither I go, thou shalt with me.*
Whichever is correct, this is clearly an invocation of Ruth 1:16, where Ruth insists on following Naomi even though she has no assurance of a life in Judah. In light of the fact that Orfeo is a king, this is a particularly interesting invocation, since David the great king of Judah was the great-grandson of Ruth (Ruth 4:17), and there was a Rabbinic legend (surely false) that Ruth herself was the daughter of Eglon king of Moab. Thus such a statement is very appropriate for a royal.

[114] Bennett/Gray, pp. 142-143, make the interesting observation that the capture of Euridice here does not at all resemble the classical Orpheus legend — but does somewhat resemble the story of Hades/Pluto's capture/rape of Persephone. Since there are many tales of Elves taking mortal women, however, we cannot assume dependence.

[115] Schiltrom ("scheltrom" in the original): A shield-wall, a rank of armed men, a phalanx. It was the formation used by the Scots at the Battle of Bannockburn. The idea is that there is no gap in the rank of arms for an enemy to break through. This is the reading of Auchinleck; Harley gives the line as "There they made watch on every side"; Ashmole, perhaps working from a defective original, can offer nothing better than "What aventour is betyde."

[116] The reference to parliament choosing a king is an interesting anachronism as well as a sign that *Sir Orfeo* is not directly translated from a French romance. Although the world *parliament* is French, the French version never chose a king! Nor, at the time *Sir Orfeo* was written, was parliament expected to choose the English king — but the Old English *witan* had had some power to choose a new king, and the barons still ended up making choices in times of a difficult succession such as when Richard I died. So, even though parliament did not function in this way at this time, the use of the word shows that the story is written from an English perspective.

[117] This image is of the "wild man of the woods," a surprisingly common theme in this era. "Wild people may be persons who have deserted civilization for one reason or another, like the early Christian saints living in the desert, 'hairy anchorites' whose

only clothing was the long body-hair which they grew; and also like those wise men driven so mad by the corruption of civilization that they sought refuge in the woods" (Samuel Kinser, "Wildmen in Festival, 1300-1550," Nicolaisen, p. 147). Thus Orfeo is here being portrayed as a type surprisingly common in the festivals of the period.

[118] Rock: Middle English *roche* in both instances in this section. Most interpreters read this as "rock," and make it a magical entrance, but Stevens, p. 116, suggests that it is a cave, or even a hill, offering the romance *Yonec* as a possible parallel.

[119] I cannot help but think that there was a stage in the tale where the King of Faërie curses Orfeo here — perhaps (a wild guess) that he enjoy his wife but be childless, since, as we shall see, Orfeo and Heurodis will have no heirs. But there is no sign of this in either the Auchinleck text ("of hir ichil þatow be bliþe") or Rumble's text from Ashmole ("I wyll that thou be of hyr blyth"); Harley here reads "Ichil þatow of hir be bliþe," according to Zielke, p. 109 (line 469).

[120] *Winchester* is the reading of Auchinleck, and I follow it because it is the reading of Sisam, but here the reading *Traciens* (Thrace) of Ashmole is surely to be preferred (and is adopted by Zielke, p. 110); Harley has "Crassens."

[121] The whole story of the return bears significant similarities to Odysseus's return in the *Odyssey*, notably in the secrecy with which Orfeo attempts to discover what has happened while he was in exile. Direct dependence is unlikely, however, since the *Odyssey* was largely lost to the west at this time because of the loss of knowledge of Greek. If there is any linkage, it would be through one of the Latin tales of Troy. However, "king-in-disguise" tales were popular in the medieval period. Indeed, there was a true tale of King Richard I in disguise, although that did not turn out well at all — he was captured and taken prisoner; John Gillingham, *Richard the Lionheart*, Times Books, 1978, p. 223.

[122] The final lines "Thus com sir Orfeo out of his cares, God graunt ous alle wele to fare" is that of Auchinleck; Harley finishes with "Amen Amen for charyte, Lord us graunt that it so be"; Ashmole offers "And that it may so be, Prey we all for Charyte." Laskaya/Salisbury and Burrow/Turville-Petrie conclude the poem with an "Amen!" Rumble, Sisam, Sands, and Tolkien omit. The addition of a terminal "Amen" is amazingly common in old texts — we find it, e.g., in a dozen or more Biblical books. Examples from Bruce M. Metzger, *A Textual Commentary on the Greek New Testament*, A Companion Volume to the United Bible Societies' Greek New Testament (Third Edition), United Bible Societies, 1971, include the ending of Matthew (p. 72), of Luke (p. 191), of 1 Corinthians (p. 571), of 2 Corinthians (p. 588), and most of the other epistles.

[123] Child, volume I, pp. 215-217. Also in Lyle, p. 63.

[124] Also in Lyle, p. 63.

[125] Lyle, pp. 63-65.

[126] Lyle, p. 66, points out that the Scottish Orpheus romance uses the name Isabel. It is thus likely, first, that the name "Isabel" preceded "Lisa Bell," and second, that the ballad took the name from this romance. But that also implies that the Scottish version is, if anything, more recent than *Sir Orfeo*.

[127] Lyle, p. 75, however thinks the meaning of the word uncertain, and suggests a connection with the harmony of the seasons, or perhaps a healing music.

[128] Nygard, p. 3.

[129] Lindahl, p. 69, observes that this has always been assumed in the case of the "Loathly Woman" type tale, but points out that it has not been proved. There is always the possibility that the ballad, or its ancestor, inspired the romances. After all, Chaucer took folktales and improved them to become his romances!

[130] First learned about in Richard Dawkins, *The Ancestor's Tale*, 2004 (references are to the 2005 Mariner Books paperback edition), especially pp. 250-251; a lot of the same material (some of it by the present author) can be found on the Internet.

[131] Dr. Stephen C. Carlson, *The Text of Galatians and Its History*, Ph.D. Thesis, Duke University, 2012. Dr. Carlson also kindly discussed the matter extensively in private communications.

[132] For which see the demonstration in Dawkins, pp. 126-133.

[133] "Tree: a connected GRAPH of which the diagram is tree-shaped in that there are no loops or paths leading from any vertex back to itself. It is a ROOTED tree if one vertex is distinguished as the ROOT or origin"—[E. J. Borowski & J. M. Borwein], *The Collins Dictionary of Mathematics*, second edition, 1989; second edition, Collins, 2002, p. 573.

[134] Ed Cray points out how fairies steal mortals repeatedly in folklore: See Stith Thompson, *Motif Index of Folk Literature*, Vol. VI, (Bloomington: Indiana University Press, 1958; motifs P424.4, R112.3, R16.3, F310 ff., and N661. See also the index of Emily Lyle, *Fairies and Folk: Approaches to the Scottish Ballad Tradition*, Sigrid Rieuwerts, ed, Vol. I (Wissenschaftlicher Verlag Trier, 2007.)

[135] Stith Thompson, *The Folktale*, University of California Press, 1946, 1977, p. 265.

[136] Some would go so far as to deny that something written can *have* a tradition. But it is well established that many texts (e.g. *Piers Plowman* or the New Testament) have "local texts." The difference between written tradition and oral tradition might better be described as the difference between a trained tradition and an untrained—but a "trained tradition" describes a minstrel tradition just as much as a written process of reproduction. Albert Lord's statement here is relevant: "Yet after all that has been said about *oral* composition as a technique.... it seems that the term of greater significance is *traditional*. Oral tells us 'how,' but traditional tells us 'what,' and even more, 'of what kind' and 'of what force'" (Albert B. Lord, *The Singer of Tales*, Harvard University Press, 1960, p. 220).

[137] G. Malcolm Laws, Jr. *American Ballads from British Broadsides: A guide for students and collectors of traditional song*, Publications of the American Folklore Society, 1957

[138] See, for example, Guthrie T. Meade, Jr., Dick Spottswood and Douglas S. Meade, *Country Music Sources*, Chapel Hill: Southern Folklife Collection, University of North Carolina, 2002.

[139] Child, #154, volume III, pp. 227-233.

¹⁴⁰ See the extensive documentation amassed by Norm Cohen, *All This for a Song*, Chapel Hill: Southern Folklife Collection, University of North Carolina, 2009 passim.

¹⁴¹ Tolkien, Gordon, & Davis, p. 69.

¹⁴² Maldwyn Mills, editor, *Ywain and Gawain, Sir Percuvell of Gales, The Anturs of Arther*, Everyman's Library, 1992, p. 102.

¹⁴³ "This suggests a wide oral transmission of the poem by minstrels, resulting in much variation when the texts came to be set down." Chris Fletcher with Roger Evans and Sally Brown: *1000 Years of English Literature: A Treasury of Literary Manuscripts*, Harry N. Abrams, no date.

¹⁴⁴ The history of this line is of note to students both of folklore and of that apostle of medieval English romance, J. R. R. Tolkien. See Shippey, pp. 180-181 (and, indeed, the whole chapter "When All Our Fathers Worshipped Stocks and Stones").

¹⁴⁵ Starting from Zielke's text, I looked at lines 1-100. My count, based on a somewhat casual inspection (I did not attempt to classify the variants), was that there were 176 variants in these 100 lines. In 76, Ashmole went against Zielke's text, in 56, the odd MS out was Harley; in four cases, Auchinleck. There were only eight places where Harley and Ashmole agreed against Auchinleck; in 32 places, all three sources disagreed. Comparison across traditions is always difficult, especially in the absence of a stemma, but this feels like at least three times the rate of divergence in, say, an equivalent section of the Greek New Testament.

¹⁴⁶ The *Gest of Robyn Hode*, Child #117, Child, Volume III, pp. 39-89; *Robin Hood and the Monk*, Child #119, Volume III, pp. 94-101; *Robin Hood and the Potter*, Child #121, Volume III, pp. 108-115.

¹⁴⁷ E.g. "Crow and Pie," Child #111; cf. Nygard, pp. 5-6.

¹⁴⁸ Lindahl, p. 68.

¹⁴⁹ John W. Hales and Frederick J. Furnival, editors, assisted by F. J. Child, W. Chappell, and others, *Bishop Percy's Folio Manuscript: Ballads and Romances*, Volume I, N. Trübner & Co., 1867. (Available on Google Books). "Lord Barnard..." is on p. 119. This piece is more commonly known as "Little Musgrave and Lady Barnard" or "Matty Groves"; Child #81.

¹⁵⁰ Hales & Furnival vol. I, p. 79; this is "Captain Car, or, Edom o Gordon," Child #178.

¹⁵¹ Hales & Furnival vol. I, p. 508; this is "King John and the Bishop," Child #45.

¹⁵² Hales & Furnival, vol. I p. 19; Child #122.

¹⁵³ Hales & Furnival, vol. I, p. 341.

¹⁵⁴ Hales & Furnival, vol. I, p. 417

¹⁵⁵ Hales & Furnival, vol. I, p. 142.

[156] i.e. "Sir Eglamore of Artois." John W. Hales and Frederick J. Furnival, editors, *The Percy Folio of Old English Ballads and Romances, Vol. III*, de la More press, 1907 (available on Google Books), p. 9.

[157] Hales & Furnival, vol. III, p. 58.

[158] Thomas Ohlgren, *Robin Hood: The Early Poems, 1465-1560, Texts, Contexts, and Ideology*, University of Delaware Press, 2007, p. 70.

[159] Hahn, p. 84.

[160] See the information at the Digital Index of Middle English Verse, under Balliol College MS 354 (http://www.cddc.vt.edu/host/ imev/Records.php? MSS=OxfBal354, checked Nov. 17. 2012).

[161] Burnley and Wiggins, page http://auchinleck.nls.uk/ contents.html.

[162] Hahn, p. 310.

[163] Child, volume I, p. 188, declares that the ballad "Hind Horn" "gives little more than the catastrophe" of the Horn romance.

[164] Child, volume V, p. 175, points out that the ballad includes only the scene of Floris saving Blancheflour. Child however notes that the incident in the ballad is not found in that form in the English versions of the romance.

[165] Deiter Mehl, *The Middle English Romances of the Thirteenth and Fourteenth Centuries*, Taylor & Francis, 2010, p. 33.

[166] Sands, pp. 279-280.

[167] Bruce Dickins & R. M. Wilson, editors, E*arly Middle English Texts*, 1951; revised edition, Bowes & Bowes, 1952, p. 44.

[168] Dickins/Wilson, p. 43.

[169] Dickins/Wilson, p. 44.

[170] Stevens, p. 45.

[171] Child, volume V, p. 175.

[172] Sands, p. 15.

[173] Sands, p. 16.

[174] Child, volume I, p. 187.

[175] Bertrand H. Bronson, *The Traditional Tunes of the Child Ballads*, 4 volumes, Princeton University Press, 1959–1972, volume I, p. 254.

[176] For Child's comments see note 163.

[177] Sands, p. 249.

[178] S. H. Steinberg, *Five Hundred Years of Printing*, 1955; new edition revised by John Trevitt, The British Library/Oak Knoll Press, 1996, p. 58.

[179] This can be seen in Copeland's work on *The Gest of Robyn Hode*, where Copeland took a de Worde original and updated the wording substantially; see the present author's own work on the *Gest*.

[180] Ward & Waller, p. 288.

[181] Sands, p. 249.

[182] Nygard, p. 16, points to the Finnish *Kalevala*, an epic assembled from ballad-like sources, but also to Spanish instances of ballads made from romances.

[183] Ward & Waller, p. 295.

[184] Nygard, p. 3.

[185] Thanks to Susan Friedman for information about several items on the list.

[186] The list of editions is not intended to be comprehensive. A good source for editions of romances is the University of York's "Database of Middle English Romance" page, http://middleenglishromance.org.uk/. Site checked October 10-November 8, 2012.

[187] Sands, pp. 279-309.

[188] TEAMS, or TEAching of the Middle Ages, is sponsored by the Consortium for the Teaching of the Middle Ages, and "is affiliated with the Medieval Institute of Western Michigan University at Kalamazoo." Their works appeared originally in book form, but are now available online at http://www.lib.rochester.edu/camelot/teams/tmsmenu.htm (site checked December 17, 2012). This is probably the largest archive of modern editions of Middle English romances in existence.

[189] The link between the *Lai* and "Fair Annie" was noted by Child and emphasized by Nygard, p. 4.

[190] The connection between the *Libeaus Desconus* and the *Laidley Worm* was suggested by Joseph Ritson, editor, revised by Edmund Goldsmid, *Ancient English Metrical Romances*, volume II, E. & G. Goldsmid, 1885 ("Digitized by Google"), p. 35. Child denied the *Laidley Worm* ballad status, printing it in an appendix to "Kemp Owyne" (Child #34), but there are some indications that it was genuinely traditional. In any case, it is another instance of a ballad involving only part of a romance.

[191] In addition to these editions, there are two full critical editions. That of Zielke, cited above,, gives an edited text based mostly on Auchinleck with the variants of the other two MSS. in the apparatus along with critical notes in German; A. J. Bliss, editor, *Sir Orfeo*, Oxford University Press, 1954, prints the three MSS in parallel columns and is considered the definitive edition.

[192] It is interesting to note that the famous ballad scholar MacEdward Leach in 1937 edited *Amis and Amiloun* for the Early English Texts Society.

[193] The result is usually regarded as a religious poem, but Turville-Petre, p. 122, declares that Susanna becomes a romance heroine in the poem — a "maiden in the Garden" — so I include it, with much hesitation, among the romances.

[194] For the reference in the Paston Letters to the *Book of the Seven Sages*, see H. S. Bennett, *Chaucer and the Fifteenth Century*, being Volume II, Part I of the *Oxford*

*History of English Literature,* Oxford, 1947; corrected reprint, 1954, p. 123. Richard Hill's MS. is Oxford, Balliol College 354; see the description in the list of manuscripts.

[195] Bennett, p. 316.

[196] Chaucer/Benson, p. 890.

[197] Those seeking more information on manuscripts might wish to begin with The Digital Index of Middle English Verse (DIMEV), http://www.cddc.vt.edu/host/imev/Index.html. Much of the information on manuscript contents comes from this site. Checked Nov. 11-14, 2012.

[198] For full information on this manuscript, see the print version of Shuffleton, *Codex Ashmole 61.*

[199] For information on this manuscript, see J. O. Halliwell, *Some Account of The Vernon Manuscript, a volume of Early English Poetry preserved in The Bodleian Library,* John Russell Smith, 1848, available on Google Books. Halliwell would date it before 1350.

[200] Cited in the Chaucer/Benson apparatus as Ra⁴.

[201] For information on the two MSS. from Gonville and Caius College, see Rev. J. J. Smith, *A Catalogue of The Manuscripts in the Library of Gonville and Caius College, Cambridge,* Cambridge University Press, 1849, available on Google Books. MS. 174 is described on pp. 86-89; MS. 175 is on pp. 89-91.

[202] A detailed description of this manuscript can be found in Montague Rhodes James, *The Western Manuscripts in the Library of Trinity College, Cambridge,* volume III, Cambridge University Press, 1902, p. 298 (available on Google Books).

[203] For this manuscript, see note 158; also [no author listed], *A Catalogue of the Manuscripts Preserved in The Library of The University of Cambridge,* Volume II, Cambridge University Press, 1857, p. 167-169 (available on Google Books).

[204] For this manuscript, see *A Catalogue of the Manuscripts Preserved in The Library of The University of Cambridge,* pp. 286-290. The manuscript was almost certainly completed before the deposition of Henry VI in 1461.

[205] For this manuscript, see *A Catalogue of the Manuscripts Preserved in The Library of The University of Cambridge,* pp. 404-408.

[206] For this manuscript, see *A Catalogue of the Manuscripts Preserved in The Library of The University of Cambridge,* pp. 505-509.

[207] This is considered one of the most important manuscripts of the *Canterbury Tales,* and is even more important for some other Chaucer poems; it is often cited in the apparatus as Gg. It is the subject of a publication, Frederick J. Furnivall, editor, *The Cambridge MS. of Chaucer's Canterbury Tales,* Chaucer Society, Trübner & Co, 1868 (available on Google Books).

[208] For this and other Oxford manuscripts, see now the Early Manuscript site at Oxford University site, http://image.ox.ac.uk. Richard Hill's MS may be accessed directly by visiting the page at http://image.ox.ac.uk/show?collection=balliol&manuscript=ms354. Site checked Dec. 26, 2012.

Robert B. Waltz received his bachelor's degree in physics and mathematics from Hamline University in 1985, and has been involved in folk music for most of his life. In 1996, he became the founding editor of The Traditional Ballad Index, a free online bibliography and reference for folk songs of English-speaking nations. His previous book include The Minnesota Heritage Songbook and the Gest of Robyn Hode. He currently works at cataloging the collections of the Ramsey County Historical Society, and shares a home with several acoustic instruments and many thousand books.

CPSIA information can be obtained at www.ICGtesting.com
Printed in the USA
LVOW10s1746310713

345111LV00015B/523/P